570

❧ ❧ ❧ ❧

ROBERT BRUCE:
King of Scots

Other Biographies by

NINA BROWN BAKER

❦ ❦ ❦ ❦

HE WOULDN'T BE KING:
THE STORY OF SIMÓN BOLIVAR

JUAREZ, HERO OF MEXICO

PETER THE GREAT

SUN YAT-SEN

GARIBALDI

LENIN

WILLIAM THE SILENT

ROBERT BRUCE:

KING OF SCOTS

By NINA BROWN BAKER

New York · The Vanguard Press, Inc.

Manufactured in the United States of America

BY H. WOLFF BOOK MANUFACTURING COMPANY,

NEW YORK, N. Y.

FOR

WINIFRED JACKSON GROOS

In Gratitude

❦ ❦ ❦ ❦

ROBERT BRUCE:
King of Scots

THE MAID OF NORWAY was dead. Whether by natural illness, by shipwreck, or by murder is not known, and can never now be known.

She sailed from her father's realm of Norway in October of 1291, on a great ship gaily decked for a princess who was to be both bride and queen. Somewhere in the treacherous waters about the Orkney Islands, the ship disappeared. Many months later, a girl child's body in a sealed casket was returned to Norway and buried in the royal crypt. So much is certain, and no more. Her death opened the bloodiest and most glorious chapter in Scottish history.

Maid Margaret was heiress to the throne of Scotland through her dead mother, wife of Norway's king and daughter of the Scot, Alexander III.

Scotland at this time was an independent kingdom on which Edward I of England had long cast covetous eyes. The simplest and cheapest way to obtain it, he thought,

1

was to marry his young son to the Scottish heiress. The match had been arranged. Margaret, not quite eight years old, was on the way to her wedding as well as her coronation when the dark waters of oblivion closed over her.

The Maid's death threw the Scottish kingdom into confusion. Alexander III had left no other direct heir, but there was a swarm of cousins, all descended from King David I, founder of the line. Each of these considered himself entitled to the vacant throne. Ugly whispers went about that one, or several, of these claimants had contrived the death of the child queen. There is no proof.

Of the claimants, thirteen in all, two finally emerged as the leading contenders. They were John Baliol of Galloway and Robert Bruce of Annandale.

Both men had their supporters among the Scottish lords. Each of them, according to the custom of the times, had a fair-sized private army.

At first it looked as though the situation might break into civil war. To avert this, a highly respected bishop suggested arbitration. He persuaded the contenders to lay their claims before Edward I, King of England, and to agree to accept his decision as final.

King Edward went about his task with a fine show of impartiality. He called for documents from all the claimants. He saw to it that the case was discussed in the English Parliament, and he summoned a special conference of Scottish nobles and clergy to render their opinion. The English Parliament announced that it was content to leave the matter to Edward's own judgment. After he came in person to Scotland, with a strong army at his back, the Scottish advisers reached the same decision.

For the great event, Edward settled himself with much state at Berwick, now on the English side of the Border, but then a Scottish seaport. There, on November 17, 1292, he gave the long-awaited verdict.

❧ The great hall of Berwick Castle was jammed long before the King made his appearance. English men-at-arms in full armor lined the bare stone walls, their weapons threateningly in view. The Scottish chieftains, as they filed in with their followers, ranged themselves in groups about their standards, so that soon the floor was a sea of waving silken banners. An empty armchair on a raised platform was the only seat, for no man sat in the presence of the King.

The Bruce battle flag, with its crossed bars, floated over three men named Robert de Brus, or Robert Bruce, as modern usage has it. They were grandfather, father, and son. It was the grandfather who was the claimant. Grandfather Bruce, known as the Competitor, is important in history because he claimed the throne. Grandson Bruce is important because after incredible struggles he ascended that throne as King Robert I. Father Bruce, in the middle, is of no importance whatever.

They stood side by side, three anxious men who had good reason to believe that they would leave this hall in sullen defeat. Hints had trickled down to them of the way the King's decision would go.

If they still hoped, they had only to glance across the hall, where John Baliol, Lord of Galloway, held boisterous court among his large following. Baliol had dined with King Edward last night, at a select dinner party to which the Bruces had not been invited. His flushed face and loud laugh indicated that he had no fears of this morning's outcome.

Grandfather Bruce, a man of eighty-two, shifted wearily on his tottery old legs. "The King is long in coming," he complained. "It's more than an hour that we've waited here."

Young Robert Bruce laughed. "Since when was royalty punctual? Straighten your shoulders, Grandfather. Baliol must not see you droop like that. Here, take my arm beneath your cloak. Does that help?"

"You're a good boy, Robert," the old man croaked, resting his weight against the stalwart shoulder. "As you say, we must not let Baliol see our fears. But, oh, my boy, there is nothing but fear left to us! The judgment will go to Baliol. I know it."

"We're not sure, Grandfather," the boy consoled him. "And even if it does—" his young voice hardened. "Must we accept it? We have men and arms. We can fight! We can—"

"Robert!" His father pulled at his sleeve. "Are you mad? Lower your voice. Or, better still, leave off such wild talk. Who are you to talk of fighting? A young esquire, not yet a knight, never tested in battle! Who asked your views? Your grandfather is the head of our house, and I am the head after him. We do not ask counsel of children!"

"Yes, Father." Young Bruce bowed his head respectfully. He was only eighteen, and, as his father had reminded him, not yet a knight. If he thought, resentfully, that his father had fought no battles either, but had spent his life in petty political maneuverings to his own advantage, he knew better than to speak such thoughts aloud. Family discipline was strong in Scottish families, and the third Robert Bruce was a good son. He had deep affection for his grandfather, the broken old Competitor. He must have seen his father as all the world saw him, a petty tyrant at home, a servile flatterer at court. But outwardly at least he preserved the attitude of filial respect that custom ordained.

"Here they come!" A murmur went through the crowded hall as a door at the far end opened to a fanfare of trumpets. Striding majestically through the close-packed ranks, surrounded by a guard of English knights, Edward I made his way to the waiting arm-chair. As he turned to face them, the entire assembly knelt, hands clasped in the gesture of fealty.

He was a magnificent figure, this Plantagenet king of England. The white tunic stretched across his broad chest bore the royal arms emblazoned in gold; his ermine-bordered velvet robe swept the floor. Now in his fifty-third year, he had behind him a record of military accomplishment that taxed the skill of the hundred minstrels he hired to sing his praises.

By any standard, Edward I was an extraordinary man. He had distinguished himself in the Crusades, spending two victorious years in Palestine. He had conquered and killed Llewellyn, Prince of Wales, and annexed the kingdom of Wales to England. To pacify the Welsh people he promised them a new prince, born in their country and speaking no foreign language. The new prince was his infant son, born on Welsh soil because Edward's devoted queen, Eleanor, had accompanied him on the invasion. The child, a few weeks old, certainly spoke no foreign language. Since Edward's day, the eldest son of the English king has been the Prince of Wales.

Edward's tender love for Eleanor has made him the

model husband of English history. When their thirty-five years together ended with her death, he set up memorial crosses all over London, where all passers-by were commanded to halt and pray for the repose of her soul. The best known of these was Charing Cross.

Edward was a perfect husband and a fearless soldier. Some other aspects of his character are not so admirable. He was an early anti-Semite, banishing some sixteen thousand Jews from England under pain of death. He personally invented the inhuman form of execution known as drawing and quartering.

He was ambitious, cruel, treacherous, highly intelligent, and the greatest general of his day. He did not, however, fight for glory or for fun. War to him was strictly a means to an end. That end was consolidating his power as ruler over as great a territory as possible. He fought if necessary. But he greatly preferred to gain dominion by subtle scheming, by means that had at least an appearance of legality. His plan to annex Scotland by marrying his son to Maid Margaret had failed, but the Bruce-Baliol dispute had given him another chance. Edward was not the man to let such a chance slip by.

At his gracious gesture, the kneeling multitude rose and stood in respectful silence. In his deep, sonorous voice, the phrases carefully chosen to sound courteous and reasonable, he began his speech.

Unhurriedly he rehearsed the events that had caused his presence among them. Calmly he made the outrageous statement that it was only fitting he should arbitrate the conflicting claims, since he himself was in fact "Lord Paramount" of Scotland, to whom any Scottish king owed homage. He added casually that all the claimants had admitted this fact.

It was quite true that in the distant past the kings of England had been styled "Lords Paramount" of Scotland. The title had been expressly repudiated by Richard Coeur-de-Lion a hundred years before.

It is true also that the contestants had agreed to recognize Edward as Lord Paramount for the purposes of the arbitration. He had made this a condition, and all of them had consented to it. Probably none of them looked upon it as anything but an empty form. The winner was not long to remain undeceived.

Having stated the problem in general terms, the King now invited the claimants to come forward and stand before him. Only two men accepted the invitation.

Most of the weaker contenders had long since abandoned their claims. One of them, King Erik of Norway, father of the dead child queen, had not even sent a representative. A few of the others were in the hall, but they stood courteously aside as spectators. Lord John Baliol of Galloway swaggered into the King's presence, a little drunk and superbly confident. There was a pause, and then old Robert Bruce, Lord of Annandale, advanced slowly on the arm of his grandson.

King Edward silently surveyed the men before him. His purpose, known only to himself at the moment, but soon to be distressingly apparent to all the world, was to choose a puppet king who would be subservient to his wishes.

His mind was made up, and yet for a moment he hesitated. Foolish, loudmouthed John Baliol, seldom sober, still had a following of tough, blunt kinsmen who might resent his taking orders from England. Old Bruce, now, with one foot in the grave—surely this ancient dotard would cause no trouble.

Very likely Grandfather Bruce would not. Nor his bootlicking son, ever anxious to propitiate those in power. On the other hand, there was this boy upon whom the old man leaned. He, too, must be taken into account. What sort of person was he, this grandson of the old Competitor's?

The youngest Robert Bruce was no stranger to the King. The Bruce family had great estates in England, and the boy had been a page at the English court. The King, frequently away at war, knew him only as a rawboned, freckled child with a mop of carroty hair, more useful with horses and falcons than in the refined services of the dining chamber.

Now in his eighteenth year—he was born at Turnberry Castle, Carrick, on July 11, 1274—young Robert had shot up to a great height, and a corresponding width. His broad shoulders were heavily muscled; his freckled fists were enormous. The face, beneath its thatch of unruly red hair, was a good-natured one, and the blue eyes were merry. But the strong jutting nose and the craggy chin gave no promise of the pliability the king was seeking. No, there was a risk there, a threat of possible trouble to come. Better leave the decision as he had made it last night. The Baliol was the safer choice.

Gravely and judicially, in the tone of an impartial arbiter, Edward gave his verdict. John Baliol was given possession of the realm of Scotland, "saving always the rights of the King of England, when he shall choose to put them forward."

The final phrase was lost in the burst of cheering that followed mention of the long-awaited name. Under cover of the noise, the three Bruces quietly made their way from the hall.

On November 30, 1292, King John I was crowned at Scone, the ancient seat of the Scottish kings. The coronation was attended by several of the disappointed claimants, but not by Grandfather Bruce. The disheartened old man made over all his rights to his son and retired to his castle in Annandale. He died there three years later.

The second Robert Bruce was in something of a quandary. He hated the Baliols too much to live in Scotland under a Baliol king, and his father's defeat had somewhat diminished the family's prestige in England. He solved his problem by giving his Scottish estates to his son, who thus became the Earl of Carrick. Then the elder Bruce sailed for a visit to Norway, taking his pretty daughter with him. Before the year was out, he married her to the widower King Erik. He lived very happily and profitably at his son-in-law's court until a few years later, when he makes his final brief and inglorious appearance in Scottish history.

Young Robert, whatever his disappointment may have been, accepted the situation with good grace. He had talked of fighting, but that was only talk. Without the backing of his grandfather or father, he could not expect the Scots to follow him against the powerful Baliol faction supported by the English army. The new Earl of Carrick had sense enough to see this. He made his bow at King John's court, and returned cheerfully enough to the carefree life of hunting and jousting from which his grandfather's cause had called him.

It was not a bad life for a young man. His English and Scottish estates brought in a comfortable income; he had castles in both countries and could live where he chose. Actually he spent most of his time in England, where he had grown up, and where he had close personal friends. King Edward, whether from policy or genuine liking it is impossible to say, showed him great favor. Bruce received his knighthood at Edward's hands, and a commission in the Household Guard.

In the quarrels that soon broke out between Edward of England and John of Scotland, young Bruce was definitely on the English side. His reasons for taking this position are understandable. He felt that the Scottish throne should have been his grandfather's, and he had no love for the triumphant Baliols. The English king had been kind to him. Most of his life had been lived in England; his friends were there. It was surely natural enough that when war came he should take his place beside them. Natural and human though his actions were, there are Scots who do not forgive him.

❦ ❦ II ❦ ❦

KING JOHN I OF SCOTLAND was known to his subjects as
"Toom Tabard," or Empty Jacket. This is hardly fair,
for beneath the extravagantly embroidered jackets he
affected there was a tiny spark of manliness, feeble
though it was, and soon extinguished. Edward did not
believe in the spark. It did not take him long to put it
out.

He began with a Christmas treat for his English court,
less than four weeks after John's coronation. The luck-
less Scot was summoned to England, there to do public
homage for his new kingdom. He was ordered to bring
with him the National Records, public documents dealing with royal births, deaths, and marriages. These
records were promptly—and accidentally, Edward
claimed—destroyed by fire.

If Edward did not arrange this accident, he certainly profited by it. With the records gone, all legal claims
to the Scottish throne, John's among them, were wiped

13

out. He could no longer claim that he was king because of his relationship to the late Alexander III, for there was no way of proving that relationship. He was king now, not by right of royal descent, but simply by the gracious favor of Edward, King of England and Lord Paramount of Scotland.

The foolish John Baliol may have thought that this was an unimportant technicality. He was soon undeceived. Edward, having made sure that everyone knew who was master of Scotland, proceeded to drive the lesson home.

Poor John had scarcely returned to his capital when new demands came from England. He was ordered to appear as the defendant in an English law court, where a wine merchant was suing for wines furnished to Alexander III, and never paid for. The King went, like any ordinary citizen, waited around while the case was heard, and found himself the loser. He paid heavy damages, as well as the bill for liquor drunk by his predecessor.

There was a series of such demands. He was frequently summoned, as any English noble might be, to sit as Justice of the Peace, hearing police court cases of poaching and disorderly conduct. Again he was ordered to sessions of the English Parliament, with which he could have no concern. In a hundred petty ways Edward demonstrated to all the world that John was his servant, bound to come and go at his bidding.

King Empty Jacket had his little spark of pride, after all. Without sufficient resources to defy the mighty English King, he looked about for an ally, and found one.

Philip IV of France was having his own troubles with Edward. He gladly entered into an alliance with John, a proceeding which the French and Scottish monarchs believed to be a secret.

Edward had an efficient spy service at both courts; very few secrets were secret from him. However, he gave no indication that he knew of the Franco-Scottish alliance. When, in June, 1295, he declared war on France, he summoned his "loyal vassal," John, to bring a Scottish army and join him for the invasion.

This is the point at which King Empty Jacket rebelled. He wrote Edward a defiant letter, refusing to make war upon his good friend Philip and professing himself greatly shocked that Edward should do so. Further to show his defiance, he announced that he was expelling from his court all nobles who held land in England and confiscating their Scottish estates.

Edward, from the time his spies brought him word of the French alliance, had been quietly expelling Scottish nobles and confiscating their English lands, so that

John's gesture became a sort of "me too" affair when the facts came out.

Edward was not a man to content himself with gestures. He had not been too anxious to fight the French anyway. Now, with so much more to be gained by the conquest of Scotland, he gladly left the French quarrel in mid-air and turned his attention to the North. On the twenty-eighth of March, 1296, with an army and a fleet, he closed in on the Scottish seaport town of Berwick.

John Baliol, by his confiscation of lands, had alienated many of the strongest nobles. His army was formed on the feudal principle. That is, he summoned the heads of great houses to his colors, commanding them to bring their own armed followings.

Naturally enough, a noble who had just been expelled from court and had had his land taken away was neither able nor willing to obey such a summons. In addition, Baliol was personally unpopular. His slavish submission to Edward had made him a laughingstock. Aside from his own numerous relatives, very few Scots cared to risk their lives to maintain his shaky throne.

Berwick put up the best defense that could be managed, but the outcome was never in doubt. The English poured in after two days' fighting and sacked the town with inhuman cruelty. Some seven thousand townsmen—

men, women, and children—were put to the sword; houses and shops were looted and burned. It was the decisive victory of the short war, although some of Baliol's kinsmen fought bravely and hopelessly for a few months longer.

Baliol himself did no fighting. In July of the same year he surrendered himself to Edward, signing a document in which he said that the English King did right to withdraw his kingdom from him, and that he resigned of his own free will, begging that his sins might be forgiven him.

Edward treated the fallen puppet with contemptuous leniency. Baliol was sent to a comfortable manor house in England, where he was allowed to hunt and live the life of a country gentleman. Later, when Wallace proclaimed himself Guardian of Scotland in King John's name, the ex-King was imprisoned in the Tower. The Pope interceded for him and found him a home in France. He lived there, cozily enough, until his death in the year after the battle of Bannockburn.

So, in less than four years, ended the unhappy reign of King Empty Jacket. The throne of Scotland was vacant again.

This time, however, Edward of England did not intend to encumber himself with puppets. He proclaimed that Scotland as a nation no longer existed but had become merely the northern counties of England. He found three chests of royal records that John had overlooked and sent them home. There, like the first lot, they were "accidentally" destroyed. Edward also appropriated the royal dinner service and the royal crown. Even more important was his seizure of the Black Rood of St. Margaret and the Stone of Scone.

The Black Rood was a religious relic, believed to be a fragment of the cross on which Christ died. It was a sacred charge of the Scottish nation. The "Crowning Stone," seven centuries old, was the actual throne, the rude seat, upon which every Scottish monarch had been crowned. The Stone is now set into the supports of the British throne in Westminster Abbey. The British king, when he receives his crown of the United Kingdom, sits upon the ancient Stone of Scone, as did the kings of Scotland before him.

Edward, having possessed himself of the outward and visible symbols of Scottish rule, next convoked a great assembly at Berwick, commanding that all landowners in the realm attend and swear fealty to him. They did this the more willingly, since he graciously restored to their original owners such lands as Baliol had confiscated.

In all, some two thousand landowners, many of them heads of religious orders, bent the knee and signed the document Edward presented to them. The document, known as the Ragman Roll because of the number of ribboned seals dangling from it, recognized Edward as the lawful ruler. The signers swore, in the words of the oath, "to become your man from this day forth, of life and limb, and to hold faith to you for the lands I claim to hold of you."

Among the signers were Robert Bruce II and Robert Bruce III. Father Bruce had come back from Norway not long before and had had himself appointed Governor of Carlisle, in northern England. No one blames the old gentleman for his signature, for he acted as always, to his own best advantage. It would have been amazing if he had done otherwise.

His son's action is a different matter. Robert Bruce, Earl of Carrick, did take the oath of allegiance to his country's conqueror. Ten years later he was to break that oath and take up arms against the man he had sworn to serve. Those are plain facts, not to be denied. His enemies have made the most of them.

Such defense as can be offered for him rests upon the nature of the oath itself. The oath of fealty was not exactly the romantic vow unto death that the old stories of chivalry make it appear. Actually, it was nothing more nor less than a real-estate transaction.

In theory, all land belonged to the king. A noble "held" his land by the king's favor, and in return he promised faithful service to his royal master. A son was required to take his own pledge before he could inherit his father's estate. The oath was a practical business contract, entered into by two parties, each of whom expected some material benefit from it.

Like all contracts, this one could be broken, or terminated, when either party failed to live up to it. King Edward himself held estates in France, for which he had sworn fealty to the French king. Whenever he felt like it, he "denounced" his oath and made war on the French. Over and over we read of nobles and clerics who "denounced" their oaths, for good reasons or for bad ones. The act never carried the stigma that some modern writers attach to it.

In Bruce's case, the Scots blame him for taking the oath, and the English for breaking it. Whether or not he was at fault over the oath, there is no denying that, for a Scottish patriot, in the beginning he was on the wrong side of the struggle. But he was very young, and the struggle had not yet taken definite shape. He was not the first national hero to be a little slow in seeing the light. Few others, once having seen it, have thrown themselves so wholeheartedly into the battle for liberty.

That time, for Bruce, had not yet come. With a clear conscience he pledged his support to King Edward and went back to the pleasant pursuits of peace.

He had a young Scottish wife whom he had married in October, 1295. Isobel, daughter of the Earl of Mar, was a relative by marriage of the Baliols. We know nothing whatever about her, nor the reason why Bruce had chosen his bride from among the enemy clan. The chances are that his father chose her for him, with some hazy idea of combining the Bruce-Baliol claims if opportunity offered. This, however, is only conjecture.

Isobel died while her husband was at Berwick, leaving him an infant daughter, Marjorie. Even her place of burial is unknown. Throughout the recorded story of Bruce's life there are such gaps, impossible to fill in. The writers of his time and immediately after covered roll on roll of parchment with his deeds of valor, with endless tedious details of battles and campaigns. Only here and there we catch imperfect glimpses of the man's personal life. A great deal is known of the second wife, Elizabeth. But for poor young Isobel, who experienced marriage, childbirth, and death within a single year, there is nothing but those bare facts.

Bruce went home to England, to his motherless child, and left the Scots to accustom themselves to their new master. For a little time he passes from the picture, and

another takes his place. On the Scottish horizon a new
star was rising, the glorious, tragic star of William Wallace. While it flamed in the startled heavens, history took
little note of the commonplace young Earl of Carrick.

❦ ❦ III ❦ ❦

MOST OF THE GREAT NOBLES of Scotland accepted Edward's assumption of authority without open protest. He was at some pains not to make their surrender too humiliating. They were left in possession of their property, although he did establish English garrisons under English officers in their castles.

The governor he appointed to rule for him, the Earl of Surrey, was a fat, jolly gentleman who was well known and well liked by those Scots who had spent much time in England. The chiefs who had actually fought in Baliol's cause were in English prisons, or dead. Edward had no reason to think that the others, whom he had treated so generously, would cause him any trouble.

Besides the landed gentry, there was one other aristocratic class in the Scotland of Bruce's day. The higher clergy, bishops and heads of monastic orders, took an active part in politics and government. They served, of course, the Roman Catholic Church, for the time was two hundred years before the Protestant Reformation.

The head of an important diocese or monastery was the equal of any lord, in both wealth and power. King Edward did not overlook the clergy when he made his heavy hand felt in Scotland. Bishops and abbots were required to sign the Ragman Roll. And, just as he filled Scotland's castles with English soldiers, so he sent English priests and monks to keep an eye on the Scottish religious establishments.

Bishop Wishart of Glasgow did not like this proceeding. He did not, as a matter of fact, like anything about King Edward, and he was furious at the Englishman's calm appropriation of the Scottish realm. The good Bishop made some cautious inquiries and found that many of the lords shared his resentment, although they felt helpless to do anything about it.

The Bishop was an old man, but an able and energetic one. He felt that something could be done, and must be. He found three men who shared his views. One was Sir William Douglas, who had unsuccessfully defended Berwick against Edward. One was Andrew de Moray, a young knight who had fought bravely for King Empty Jacket. The third was Sir William Wallace.

Douglas and Moray came from great houses, bearing famous names already known to history. Wallace was the younger son of a simple country gentleman, from a family originally Welsh.

There are many legends about his childhood, but almost no authentic information. He was born in 1274, the same year as the younger Bruce. Although this would make him twenty-three in 1297, when he first appears to challenge Edward's might, he was still an "esquire," the stage that preceded knighthood.

It is an odd fact that he never did become a knight by the usual formal ceremony, although his followers lovingly called him Sir William. Knighthood was bestowed by the king for meritorious service, usually on the field of battle. Until his twenty-fourth year Wallace had fought no battles. When his battles were done, the King of England vengefully devised a special and horrible mark of recognition for his part in them.

Wallace and Moray and Douglas, in the early spring of 1297, started a guerrilla campaign against Edward's garrisons in the Scottish castles. The Glasgow Bishop and the clergy under him sent them recruits, and Moray and Douglas, at least, could call on the fighting men of their own clans. Before the spring was far advanced, the rebellion had broken into a real war.

It was very different from warfare as we know it. The great stone castles, widely scattered over a sparsely inhabited land, were actually forts. The taking of one

meant victory in that section. It had no effect whatever
on the national scene. Only as the castles could be
forced to surrender, one by one, could progress be
counted.

Wallace and his friends were seldom lucky enough
to obtain possession of a castle and keep it. Their raids
were designed to kill as many Englishmen as possible,
to destroy wells and foodstocks, to create turmoil and
panic.

At this, for a time, they were highly successful. They
scattered their efforts widely, so that neither the English
officers nor the Scottish chiefs could feel sure of a moment's peace. Their first notable victory was the capture
of Lanark, in Douglas's home county, where they killed
the unpopular sheriff who collected Edward's taxes.
This brought a number of lesser nobles to the side of
Wallace and strengthened the insurgent forces by men
and money.

Edward's lieutenant for Scotland, the Earl of Surrey,
scurried home to tell his royal master of these scandal-
ous happenings. The King, very busy with preparations
for his French war, was more irritated than alarmed.
Surrey was not much of a general, but he did have a
military title. Edward was certain that he himself had
so thoroughly subdued Scotland that there was nothing
to fear from any little local uprising led by such an

unknown as Wallace. He needed his good officers in France. Surely a second-string general would do for this affair? He gave Surrey an increased army and ordered him to go back and restore order.

General Lord Surrey, an easygoing person who never fought at night because he believed that a man needs his sleep, shared the King's contempt for the rebels. He moved north at a leisurely pace, going into camp every night for eight full hours on his cherished featherbed. Early in September, 1297, he reached Stirling Bridge where it spanned the River Forth.

The bridge was a long, narrow, wooden structure of great age. Surrey approached from the south, where the land is flat. On the northern bank, however, rising steeply from the river, there is a rocky mass known as Abbey Craig.

Behind this natural fortress, well screened by trees, Wallace waited with two hundred men. They were on foot, armed with pikes, six-foot wooden spears topped with steel blades. The English strength is not known, but their numbers are said to have been at least ten times that of Wallace's little army. Most of them were mounted. The cavalry carried swords and battleaxes. There was also a corps of the famous English bowmen who had conquered Wales for Edward.

There is some evidence that Surrey's spies knew of

the Scots' presence behind the Craig, and that they reported it. If this is true, the sleepy general's actions are hard to understand. While he finished his excellent breakfast on the south bank, he sent his vanguard, a company of cavalrymen, across the bridge.

The span was so narrow that only two horsemen could ride abreast. Silent and well hidden, Wallace's men waited until the troop had left the bridge on their side and were attempting to re-form in fours for the road. Then, with bagpipes shrilling, with wild yells to confuse the horses, they poured down from the height.

The startled battle-chargers plunged wildly, and many a rider was thrown upon the waiting spears. While the fight raged, picked men with axes were busy at the northern supports of the bridge. The flimsy structure rocked and sagged into the swift waters below.

Surrey and the main army, watching helplessly from the safety of the south bank, saw their comrades go down in bloody defeat.

They were still far stronger in numbers and arms than the Scots, and rivers have been forded to turn the tide of other battles. Whether Surrey gave the order to retreat, or whether he was unable to check a sudden panic, it is impossible to say. The English army fled, leaving all their possessions behind them. None fled faster than the noble Earl of Surrey, for he arrived first at the near-by stronghold of Berwick, on a horse so far spent that "it was never able to eat corn again," to quote a man whose father was there.

Stirling Bridge was the first pitched battle of Wallace's career, and his most brilliant victory. He was saddened by the loss of young Moray, who received his death wound on the bridge. All else was gain. Everywhere across the land, Scots began to take heart, to believe that they need not, after all, bow meekly to the English yoke. From all sides, chiefs came in with men and money. Wallace, an unimportant young rebel, had suddenly become a national hero, the man who was to make Scotland free.

He might, perhaps, have made himself king in the process, as other successful revolutionists have done. But William Wallace was a Scot, with a deep respect for law and tradition. John Baliol, legally crowned King of Scotland, had been deposed by force. Immediately following the victory at Stirling, Wallace proclaimed himself Guardian of Scotland, on behalf of King John.

For a little time, it looked as though he would actually succeed in restoring the Baliols to power. John himself was a prisoner in England, but he had plenty of relatives in Scotland free to accept Wallace's generous support of the family. It goes without saying that they did accept it.

And now comes one of those passages that plague the truthful biographer. While young William Wallace was gallantly building his forlorn hope into a real prospect of Scottish independence, what was Robert Bruce doing? The frank answer is that he was doing nothing very commendable.

In the early days of Wallace's struggle, Bruce had offered some help. From time to time, as it went on, he tentatively gave his assistance, only to return later to his English allegiance. He did not come out wholeheartedly as a Wallace partisan until after the victory at Stirling Bridge raised high hopes of the restoration of the Scottish throne.

Somewhere in these "double-dealings" that cloud Bruce's younger days it might be possible to find the hand of his father. The old gentleman, father-in-law of Norway's king and governor of Carlisle by royal favor, was quakingly anxious to do nothing that would worsen his comfortable position. But, on the other hand, one would have a still finer position if one could become king of Scotland—an office to which the Bruces certainly had a legitimate claim. If Wallace, this upstart from nowhere, really had power to restore the throne, why not correct the wrong that Edward had done and set the rightful claimant upon it?

For contact with the rebels, there was the young Earl

of Carrick, a dutiful son who could be trusted to advance his father's interests. And who, if things went badly, could always be repudiated. "A hot-headed youth," he could tell the King, "headstrong and foolish. Surely your Majesty would not blame his father, who, as you know, has always been your most devoted servant?"

So the old courtier may have reasoned. This is pure guesswork. There is no way of knowing whether Robert acted on his father's behalf or strictly on his own, when he first espoused Wallace's cause and then abandoned it.

Only one undisputed fact makes the guesswork reasonable. This is the fact that all Robert's hesitancy vanished with his father's death. From that day, he pursued the dangerous road to liberty unflinchingly, heedless of difficulties and hardships. So long as old Bruce lived, his conduct needs excuses that are hard to come by. From the moment that he became "The" Bruce, head of the family, the necessity for excuses disappeared forever.

Robert Bruce, after Stirling, went over openly to the side of Wallace. So did Baliol's nephew, Red John Comyn of Badenoch. The two young men, of rival families, cannot have been friends, but they were old acquaintances. Both had achieved knighthood at Edward's court; they had many times opposed each other in the dangerous sport of the tournament.

It cannot be maintained that either of these young nobles was of much practical aid to Wallace. He sent them to raid various castles, while he himself remained in command of the good-sized army that he had been able to muster. Neither Comyn nor Bruce was present at Falkirk, Wallace's second and last full-scale battle.

Edward, shocked into action by the defeat at Stirling, had again abandoned plans for the French war and come home to handle the Scottish situation himself. He crossed the Border in July, 1298, with an army of thirty thousand. On the twentieth of that month he had word that Wallace was encamped near Falkirk, not far from the site of his Stirling triumph. There, on the morning of July 21, Edward attacked on a hillside called Slamannan Moor.

The battle of Falkirk is a notable one in military history. It marks the end of the long transition from Middle Age methods, which relied on hand-to-hand fighting, to modern warfare, which puts its chief emphasis on missiles.

The missile, in that pre-gunpowder day, was the arrow. In the hands of Edward's longbowmen it proved its deadliness. The arrow, of course, was no novelty; the Scots had archers among their ranks. But Scottish archers had only the simple shortbow and the slow crossbow. Edward's men, a massive corps of them, were plentifully supplied with the longbow, tall as a man, able to send its swift shaft through thick oak wood, or through chain mail.

Every twist and turn of this epoch-making battle is recorded in the books on military science. For us it is enough to know that it ended in victory for the English, and crushing defeat for Wallace. A third of his army was killed; the others fled or were captured. He himself, with a little handful of followers, managed to escape into the hills.

William Wallace had yet seven more years of life before his tragic end. He never ceased to fight, and he never dreamed of surrender, but his day was over. When he was not leading small raids to harass the English, he was abroad, trying to gain support from foreign rulers and the Pope. He had little luck abroad, and at home his friends melted away. The time came when his influence counted for so little that he resigned his title of Guardian of Scotland into the hands of a stanch supporter, Bishop Lamberton of St. Andrews.

Lamberton was a friend of that other patriotic bishop, Wishart, who had enlisted Wallace in the beginning. The two churchmen put their heads together, and, with the concurrence of such nobles as were available, they named two new Guardians for Scotland. These were Red John Comyn of Badenoch and Robert Bruce, Earl of Carrick.

The bishops no doubt felt that by selecting these two men for the post of honor they would reconcile the factions into a united front against the English. Their pious hopes had little foundation. Whether Comyn and Bruce had been open enemies up to this time is not known. We do know that at a council meeting shortly after their appointment the two young Guardians engaged in a fight with drawn daggers. They were separated without bloodshed, and Bishop Lamberton became third Guardian, to keep the peace between them.

The guardianship worked no better than might have been expected. It was in no sense a government, for the powerful chieftains did as they pleased. The continuous marching of armies had ruined the crops; trade was at a standstill. Scotland, never a rich land, was hungry and desolate as the long struggle dragged on.

Edward, to his disappointment, was not able to follow up his victory at Falkirk by completely subjugating the stubborn Scots. Twice, in the three uneasy years that followed, both sides agreed to a long truce. The fighting died down and flared up again, with no decisive results on either side.

Sometime during the first period of truce, Bruce resigned or was deposed as Guardian. It is supposed that by this time he—or his father—had realized that the

Baliols and Comyns were too powerful to oppose; that
any restoration could only benefit the rival house. When
the second truce was proclaimed, Bruce went back to
England. King Edward was very gracious. He forgave
him everything, bestowed some important honorary offices on him, and found him a rich wife.

The bride that Edward chose for Bruce's second wife
was Elizabeth de Burgh, whose father was the Earl of
Ulster. The Irish earl had married a Douglas, daughter
of the William Douglas who was Wallace's friend. Lady
Elizabeth was a Scotch-Irish lassie of fifteen, pretty and
very shy, with a fabulous dowry. She had grown up in
Ireland and England, and she considered Scotland a
barbarous country unfit for civilized living. Her father
and King Edward both assured her she would never have
to live there. Her husband may or may not have made
her the same promise. In after years she tearfully
claimed that he had, and that she never knew a happy
day after he callously broke it.

There is simply no way of knowing how Bruce felt
toward the whining child he married. He treated her
with unvarying gentleness when he was with her, and
seems never to have suffered any distress in her absence.
Of his love for little Maid Marjorie, daughter of his
first marriage, we have plenty of evidence. Nothing in
the sketchy records gives any hint of his real feeling for

Elizabeth. They were married in June, 1302, and the marriage endured until her death in 1327.

Edward's war with France finally came to an end, and he was able to turn all his strength against rebellious Scotland. He succeeded so well that on February 9, 1304, all the nobles except Wallace surrendered. Red John Comyn was among them.

In March of the same year Robert Bruce the elder died, leaving five sons and several daughters. Robert, the oldest son, was now "The" Bruce. He was also claimant to the throne of Scotland. He had now, as he could never have had while his father lived, unquestioned authority over a throng of brothers, cousins, and kinsmen in remote degree. For the first time in his life, he was free to act as his own judgment dictated.

❧ ❧ IV ❧ ❧

CAMBUSKENNETH ABBEY stood upon the north bank of the River Forth, not far from the site of Wallace's Stirling Bridge victory. Like most Scottish abbeys, it served as a sort of settlement house for the surrounding countryside. Classes were conducted there for the sons of farmers who aspired to learn their letters, and from the Abbey the brothers went out in what was a primitive form of social service. The sick were visited, the hungry were fed, practical counsel and religious comfort were freely available to those in need of it. Cambuskenneth, with its attached church, was a huge stone pile always humming with activity.

To the Abbey, on a summer day in 1304, came a distinguished guest. Bishop Lamberton of St. Andrews paid his visit openly, accompanied by the troop of retainers who commonly attended a dignitary of the Church. He was cordially received by the Father Abbot. After evening service he dined with the brothers in the

37

common room and then asked to be shown to his chamber, explaining that the journey had wearied him.

The Abbey kept early hours. By the time the long northern twilight had faded into darkness, the great stone chapter house was asleep. Only in the Abbey church, where a relay of monks prayed in perpetual adoration, was there a flicker of candlelight. The faint beams dimly outlined the church windows, but they did not reach the river bank, where a man crouched motionless.

To Colin, the Bishop's trusted groom, the night seemed to go on forever. Following his master's instructions, he had concealed himself in a clump of hazel bushes, invisible from the chapter-house windows. Not, as he reflected grumpily, that the poor hard-working brothers, who rose an hour before dawn, would be likely to spend time peering out into the night. But the lord Bishop had been very insistent. It was vital, absolutely vital, that his expected visitor should come and go without being seen.

It was a fine starry night, warm and still. The river below him glowed faintly silver, but the opposite shore was densely black. Colin, strain his eyes though he might, did not see the boat put out from that blackness. It was not until his ears caught the faint splash of muffled oars that he was able to pick out the small craft in midstream.

He shifted his cramped limbs with a sigh of relief. At last! Cautiously he scrambled to his feet and down to the water's edge. There were two men in the boat. One sat silently at the oars, while the other leaped lightly ashore.

No words were exchanged. The newcomer, a huge figure muffled in a monk's cloak, the cowl pulled far over his face, touched Colin's arm inquiringly. Colin nodded and led the way up the sandy bank, setting his feet carefully so as not to dislodge a betraying pebble. The stranger followed with equal caution, although the scrape of a spur sounded alarmingly loud in the stillness.

Colin slipped in at the scullery door and crossed the dark deserted kitchen. The dining hall then, with trestles and benches to be skirted in the dark, and so into a narrow corridor. From behind closed doors came an occasional snore; there was no light and no other sound.

The groom did not knock on the guest-room door. Slowly he pushed it open; when the stranger's breathing sounded beside him, he closed it silently. Then, and only then, a candle was lit beside the bed.

The Abbey's guest room, larger than the monks' cells, was no more luxuriously furnished. A magnificent carved crucifix hung over the low cot bed. There were two wooden stools. A taller stool held pitcher and basin, and the candlestick. No other furnishings softened the harsh stone walls and floor.

Bishop Lamberton rose from sleep fully clothed, a handsome, vigorous man in the early fifties. He nodded dismissingly to Colin, who slipped out without a word. The Bishop fastened the door behind him and then turned to his guest.

"We are safe now, my lord, although it is well to speak softly. May I take your cloak?"

"Thank you." The newcomer pushed back the hood and freed his massive shoulders from the cumbersome folds. He tossed the coarse brown garment carelessly on the bed and stood revealed in supple steel chain mail, the armored jerkin covered by a white linen surcoat. Well over six feet tall, he towered almost to the stone ceiling. His thick red hair, long and curling, framed a ruddy face with bright blue eyes. He had, an old chronicler tells us, "no great comeliness," but he looked every inch the fighting man.

Lamberton motioned him to a stool. "We have much to discuss, my lord of Carrick," he said gravely. "It is good of you to come at my invitation. I could have wished that our dear friend Wishart might be with us. But, as you know, his Reverence is an old man, and ailing. He is with us in spirit."

"I'd like to have seen him," Bruce said simply. "He is the finest, most saintly man I have ever known. But you wrote me that you would speak for him."

"For him, and for all of Scotland. My lord, we have little time. The fate of our unhappy country may hang upon the words exchanged between us this night. Let us be brief, and to the point."

Bruce inclined his head. "I haven't much skill in diplomatic fencing," he admitted. "It will suit me very well if you will say frankly what is in your mind, my lord Bishop."

"Um. First I'll say what's in the mind of every Scot worthy of the name. Edward of England is not, and has no right to call himself, Lord Paramount of Scotland. Oh, you need not remind me. I signed the Ragman Roll, with everyone else. What could we do? We yielded to superior force, as the bravest must. But force does not make right, my lord! It was a wicked, shameful wrong that his Majesty of England did. It is right, in the sight of God and all free men, if we undo that wrong. So far, do you agree with me? If you do not, we can end this discussion now. Speak, Sir Robert, and tell me if you agree."

For a moment his visitor was silent. Then, very carefully, he answered, "I do not wish to end the discussion,

Reverend Father. Let us assume for argument's sake that I agree with you."

The Bishop frowned. Accustomed as he was to the flaming patriotism of Wallace, he found the young man's caution distasteful. However, he went on:

"Edward's power is by no means secure here, in our broken, bleeding land. Wallace's victory at Stirling Bridge put real heart into our Scots, even though the Falkirk defeat dashed their hopes. The name of Wallace still has power to rally men, men who will fight to free their country from the tyrant's yoke. What if for the moment our cause is going badly? Wallace does not believe, and I do not believe, that our cause is lost! We think that it can still be won. We know it can be won, if every true Scot does his part!"

"And you think there is a part for me?" Bruce put in. "Is that why you summoned me here, my lord Bishop?"

Lamberton, who had been about to launch into one of those eloquent patriotic speeches of which he was master, looked a little dashed at the matter-of-fact interruption.

"Well, yes. You are thirty years old, Carrick, at the peak of youthful strength. You have great wealth, and you are the head of a fighting family which has served our country gloriously in bygone days. Are you content to live a vassal to the English king? Do you not feel that your place is beside Wallace and Douglas, beside all those Scots who have sworn to make Scotland free? If you have any spirit, any pride—"

"Reverend Father!" The young man's tone was respectful, but very firm. "I assure you it is not necessary to question the spirit and pride of a Bruce. As you say, we have little time. May I ask a practical question?"

"Ask," the cleric said briefly.

Bruce chose his words. "You speak of the cause for which Wallace fights. Is not that cause the restoration of the Baliols to the throne?"

The Bishop was not put out by the blunt inquiry.

"The cause is the restoration of the Scottish throne, free from English dominion. Surely you must remember that our king was deposed by military violence on Edward's part?"

"I remember that," Bruce answered. "My memory is very good. I also remember that John Baliol owed his throne to Edward in the first place. Are you asking me to shed my blood to restore it to him? Because if you are, you may have my answer now. I will not fight for the Empty Jacket!"

The Bishop smiled. "Will it surprise you when I say that you do not make me too unhappy? In the beginning, Wallace proclaimed himself Guardian in King John's name. This was on Wishart's advice, and mine. But nine unhappy years have passed since then, and we have had ample time to reconsider. I will be frank with you, Carrick. We have come, all of us, to the conclusion that Baliol is not worth fighting for. Neither he, nor his witless son. Does that please you?"

Bruce drew a long breath. "It does please me, I can't deny it. I thought you had sent for me to enlist me in the Baliol cause. To refuse would seem to deny the hope of a free Scotland. And yet, I had determined to refuse. Your words take a weight off my mind, Father."

"Well, that's one misunderstanding cleared up." The Bishop glanced toward the tiny window where the gray of dawn would show itself. There was blackness still, but he hurried on.

"I'll not waste words, Carrick. We do not intend to free Scotland and then find ourselves in the same dilemma as when the Maid of Norway died. This time, we're going to have a king of our own choosing—yes, chosen even before we have a throne to offer him. Oh, I'm speaking seriously! And, remember, I'm not speaking for myself alone. I have canvassed all the gentry and clergy who have taken Wallace's side. I have talked long with Wallace and Wishart. All are agreed. By John's cowardice, the Baliols have forfeited their claim. There remains then another descendant of King David I, with a right as strong as any Baliol, and we think with the character to maintain it. In the name of the Scottish people when they shall be free, my lord, I ask you to accept the crown!"

Neither surprise nor gratification showed on the calm young face. Only the heavy sandy brows came together in puzzlement. "I did not know that Scotland thought so well of me," he said at last.

The Bishop spoke a little tartly. "Perhaps, if we are to be very frank, I may say that it is rather that we think so ill of the Baliols."

Unexpectedly, Bruce put his head back and roared. Then, at his host's warning gesture, he stifled the laugh with a huge freckled hand.

"I like your frankness better than your oratory, my lord Bishop," he chuckled. "No, no apologies, please! Let's get down to business and discuss this matter like two sensible men. You say that Scotland wants me. At this minute, only one man has the right to speak for free Scots, a man who has bought that right with blood. Does William Wallace want me?"

"I've told you that he does."

"You're certain?" Bruce pressed. "The truth, please."

Lamberton hesitated a minute. Then he said, "You liked my frankness a minute ago, my lord. I'll be franker still. Wallace is puzzled, as we all are, by your conduct in the past. You were on Edward's side, on our side, on our side, on Edward's side again. We have not always felt quite certain that we could—could—"

"Could trust me?" Bruce's voice was very quiet. "I can understand that. You did not feel that you could trust me in the past. Do you feel that you can trust me in the future? Go on being frank, please."

"Candidly, then, we do not know. It is a risk we must take. Our country has suffered greatly, and will suffer more before the struggle ends. When it does end, she must have peace. A peace that can only be maintained by a strong leader, armed with the traditional authority of a legitimate king. We have chosen you as our best hope."

Bruce threw back his powerful shoulders, his broadsword clanking gently against his mailed hose. "A risk —a hope—that is how Wallace sees me, then?

"Well, so be it. What I have done in the past is done. I have no explanations to offer, and no apologies. But this one thing I pledge to you, upon the sacred honor of a Bruce. From this day forward, my lord Bishop, I will serve Scotland with all the strength God gives me. I will not stint in time, nor money, nor my life's blood. If Heaven grants me the throne of my ancestors, which I solemnly declare is my right, I will not disgrace it. Will that do?"

The Bishop bowed his head. "It will do very well, my lord King."

"Then bless me!" The knight sank to his knees. "Bless me to the service of my country, Father, for while I live I shall know no other service."

Solemnly the Bishop blessed him, a king in name only, and a king with a bloody path to travel before he reached his throne. What considerations of family pride, of selfless patriotism, or of self-interest moved him, we cannot know. If the people of Scotland risked something in their choice, Robert Bruce, too, was taking the gamble of a lifetime. Once the die was cast, he never faltered, not even when it seemed that all heaven and earth were against him.

Far away in the Abbey barnyard a cock crowed. Hastily Bruce and the Bishop concluded their talk. It was not possible, Lamberton explained, to make any immediate move. Bruce must go back to England and continue his ordinary life until the hour struck. If it was necessary to speak against the Scottish rebels, in order to avoid rousing the King's animosity, then he must do that. At all costs, the English must not know that the Scots had chosen a king to lead them out of bondage.

WILLIAM WALLACE, after some months abroad, returned to Scotland. The English King had offered a large reward for his capture, so that his stay in Glasgow was a secret one. He lodged in the house of a soldier named Ralph Ray, a vassal of Wallace's good friend Sir John de Menteith.

The infamy of his betrayal must be divided between Ray and Menteith, as the reward was divided. The soldier received forty marks. Sir John, who had been one of Wallace's earliest followers, who had supported him on many a daring raid, took the Judas-price of one hundred and fifty marks.

They hurried the prisoner to London, and to his trial at Westminster. It was held on August 22, 1305, and it was not much of a trial. The indictment was read to him, and his sentence pronounced.

He stood before his judges, straight and proud in his ragged kilt of Highland plaid. They had taken his armor from him, they had dragged him through the dusty London streets, and his face bore many a cut and bruise inflicted by his captors. Clearly and strongly he spoke the few brief words they allowed him before he was hustled off to die.

William Wallace protested that he was not a traitor, for he owned no land and therefore had never been required to swear allegiance to the English king. So much they let him say, and no more.

His simple statement was true enough and might have acquitted him of the charge of treason before a just judge. However, it would have made little difference. There were other charges, and he did not deny them. King Edward had done him the honor of personally drawing up the schedule of punishment for the crimes of which he stood convicted. Here it is, in the words of the English historian Maxwell:

"As a homicide and robber he was hanged; as an outlaw he was beheaded; for sacrilege (the burning of churches), his entrails were taken out and burnt; as a traitor, his head was fixed on London Bridge, and his quarters suspended on gibbets at Newcastle-on-Tyne, Berwick, Stirling, and Perth."

Thus, in this designedly horrible manner, died Wallace, the pure and perfect knight, the hero without blemish. Not once in his brief lifetime had he bent the knee to the oppressor; never, by word or deed, had he tarnished the glowing ideal that he followed unto death. His place is warm and secure in the hearts of his countrymen. Burns's stirring hymn, "Scots wha hae wi' Wallace bled," is forever the rallying-cry where Scottish men stand in battle. His land of Scotland is dotted with Wallace monuments, and any chance-met schoolchild will proudly recount the tale of his glory. Edward killed the man's body with fiendish thoroughness. The noble soul he could not kill grows ever stronger as the years go by, an undying inspiration to man's courage and love of country.

Wallace was dead, aften ten years of armed resistance to the English conquest. Edward, convinced that resistance died with its leader, was in a mood of calculated generosity. He released poor John Baliol and his silly son to the Pope's charity, and he gave Scotland a pretense of self-government.

A hand-picked Scottish Parliament was set up, containing ten Scots and twenty Englishmen. This body proceeded to repeal all the old laws and enact new ones. They were not bad laws. But they were made in England, after Edward's instructions, and they were enforced by new judges of his appointing. In every possible way he sought to make it clear that Scotland was now a lesser England.

To represent him as Viceroy, Edward chose his nephew, John of Brittany. He was a kindly, tactful young man, just the person to win over the resentful Scottish nobles and reconcile them to the new order.

John was at present in France, and until he could arrive the King made the gracious gesture of appointing Bishop Lamberton as chief Guardian. Edward knew that Lamberton had supported Wallace, but he hoped the Bishop would now be willing to let bygones be bygones. Lamberton accepted, giving no indication that he had other ideas.

Another Scot who was high in Edward's favor at this time was the Lord of Badenoch, Red John Comyn. Like his rival Bruce, this young man had lived down his participation in Wallace's revolt and was welcome at the English court. Again like Bruce, Comyn was in secret communication with Lamberton and Wishart, the patriotic Scottish bishops.

The initiative in this case came from him. At about the time of Wallace's death he wrote urgent letters to both churchmen, urging his claim.

As John Comyn saw it, he was his uncle Baliol's heir, and the rightful pretender to the Scottish throne. Baliol had given it up, and his son had no aspirations. There were other Baliol nephews besides Red John, but they were willing to step aside in his favor.

Comyn's case was good enough; actually as good as Bruce's, to a disinterested observer. Naturally, there were no disinterested observers about. If the Comyns were convinced of the rightness of their claim, so were the Bruces. Both men had plenty of relatives ready to back them. It was not a pleasant situation, nor one calculated to aid the desperate Scottish cause.

Wishart and Lamberton, two intelligent, earnest men who thought only of their country's good, had debated long and prayerfully over their choice of a leader. Comyn did not make his specific demand in Wallace's lifetime, but he was the logical choice if the house of Baliol was to be favored.

The Bishops found strong sentiment against Comyn among the Scottish lords, chiefly on the basis of his personality. He was sly, self-seeking, and notoriously dishonest in money matters. Scrupulous honesty was and is a virtue highly esteemed in Scotland. A long string of unpaid bills seems to have been the main factor that caused the good Bishops to reject him.

The choice of Bruce was made a year before Wallace's death. When, after the execution, Comyn wrote to the Bishops to press his claim, he also sent a secret letter to Bruce. In it he demanded his aid, "as my loyal subject," in winning the crown.

Bruce, knowing his man, responded with a practical offer. He himself, he wrote, would be Scotland's next king. But if Comyn would abandon his claim, and render assistance, he would receive all the Bruce lands and titles as his reward.

This, at least, is one version of what happened. As in so many cases, the old chronicles are in violent conflict here. Another writer has it that Bruce made the first advance, offering to buy off Comyn with all his wealth. This is certainly the story that Comyn told Edward, and it could be true. Comyn's love of money was well known; Bruce may have hoped to forestall any conflict by an extravagant bribe.

Whatever the circumstances, Comyn saw to it that the King heard of Bruce's offer. Red John did not make the revelation himself, nor was he even at court when it was done. He had his wife write a pleasant gossiping letter to her sister, who was married to one of Edward's generals. In the course of the letter, Lady Comyn casually mentioned the "infamous offer" her husband had received from Bruce and his virtuous horror that any man should tempt him to treason. The letter fell into the King's hands, as was intended.

It happened that Edward was entertaining that night, and Bruce was among his guests. The feast passed off as usual, with good food, the songs of minstrels, and plenty of strong red wine. Never had the Earl of Carrick enjoyed more attention from the King. Yet, as the banquet moved from one course to another, the young noble began to feel a distinct uneasiness.

Edward asked a great many questions, chiefly about the situation in Scotland. Did his friend Carrick think that, after all, Lamberton and those others were to be trusted? What if these treacherous Scots, pretending loyalty, were secretly plotting against their English masters? If such a plot existed, just what form did Bruce think it would take? Would they, perhaps, think of setting John Comyn on the throne? "Or even yourself, Robert," the King suggested, with a laugh to show he was joking. "Your old grandfather, now, he really thought he should have been king of Scotland. I suppose there might be some fools up there who think the same of you!"

Bruce joined in the laugh and answered as disarmingly as he could. But his uneasiness grew. The food had long since been eaten, and the company lingered at table, making merry over the wine. The crowded stuffy hall suddenly became oppressive.

On an impulse, Robert Bruce rose to his feet and begged the King's indulgence. "My secretary has just recovered from an illness, and I have many letters to write." He gave the first excuse that came into his head.

"If your Majesty will excuse me, I'll go home and dictate them now."

"Of course, of course!" the King answered heartily. "We know what a great letter-writer you are, Robert. Don't let us detain you from it."

The words were commonplace, but the accompanying laugh made them significant. More disturbed than he would have cared to admit, Bruce said good night and left the hall.

As the curtain fell behind him. Edward turned to the Earl of Gloucester at his side. The King had not slighted the wine cup; his usual wily caution was not operating. "There," he said viciously, "goes a man I intend to hang."

Gloucester was Edward's son-in-law, but he was also Bruce's cousin and friend. Although the King had been drinking, his words were spoken soberly, with a vengeful menace impossible to mistake. Gloucester needed no more to know that his friend was in deadly danger.

He racked his brain for a way to warn Bruce. To leave the table after the King's remark might excite suspicion. Surely tomorrow morning would be time enough? He stole a glance at his father-in-law's flushed, vindictive face and did not feel reassured. Somehow, at all costs, he must get word to Bruce without delay.

With an exclamation of annoyance, he bent down and

groped under the table. "These spurs!" he said crossly. "One of them has slipped off again. They're worse than useless."

He unbuckled both spurs and turned to the young page behind his chair. "Here!" he commanded. "Take the things to the man I got them from. Maybe he can do something with them."

Edwin Montgomery, the page, was only fourteen years old, but he had sharp ears and a keen mind. He had heard the King's remark. He knew quite well that the spurs had been a present to Gloucester from Bruce. Without asking any questions, he slipped off on his mission.

Bruce had no house in Westminster but stayed, when he came to court, in the home of a friend. Edwin found him there and delivered the spurs. Within an hour Bruce had taken the road for Scotland.

It was a bitter winter's night, thick with driving snow. Two riders, his secretary and a servant, were his only companions. The fugitives had a few hours to spare, for it was not until daylight that a company of archers surrounded the house he had left. They had his Majesty's warrant for the arrest of Robert Bruce, Earl of Carrick, as a traitor to the King.

Bruce and his two followers crossed the Scottish border in safety. Somewhere along the way they came upon a man in the livery of the Comyns. He was riding to Westminster, with a letter from his master to Edward.

Bruce, knowing nothing of what had aroused the King's displeasure, was suspicious enough to seize and read the letter. In it Comyn boldly confirmed his wife's gossip. He had been approached by Bruce, he said, to enter into a conspiracy to regain the Scottish crown. He had nobly spurned such plotting, even though it offered him vast wealth. He ended by recommending that Edward put the traitor to death, in the same admirable manner employed for that other rebel, Wallace.

Bruce confiscated the letter and bade the man ride back to his master with a message from him. Sitting on his horse in the snow-swept moorland, he hastily dictated a note to his shivering secretary. Matters had arisen, he said, which demanded consultation. Would his lordship of Badenoch be good enough to meet him six days hence, at Dumfries? The Church of the Minorite Friars would be a convenient meeting place, and the hour had best be midnight.

The messenger rode off, and Bruce went on to his castle of Lochmaben in Annandale. His wife Elizabeth was there, and his nine-year-old daughter Marjorie. He had, however, little leisure for family companionship.

The call went out to the four Bruce brothers, scattered in country seats throughout Carrick and Annandale.

They came clanking in battle array to Lochmaben, their men-at-arms following behind them.

Bishop Lamberton came, alarmed but exultant. He had not set this as the hour to strike, but, since fate had so decreed it, let it be. The Bishop's work had been well done. Wallace's shameful death, instead of discouraging the patriots, had roused them to a new pitch of wrath. All over Scotland, men were waiting for the word.

That word Bruce was ready to give. From this day forward it would be the Scots against the English, a war that could end only in triumph or in annihilation. From some secret hiding place the Bishop brought out the old forbidden royal flag, with its lion among the scarlet lilies. Under it his people swore to follow Robert Bruce to victory or death.

Gravely, solemnly, the young King-to-be accepted the pledges that poured in. Scot against Englishman, then, and no turning back. But first there was a little matter that must be settled, an issue of Scot against Scot.

On February 10, 1306, taking his brothers with him, Bruce rode down to Dumfries, to the mellow old church of the Minorite Friars.

❧ ❧ VI ❧ ❧

ROBERT BRUCE and Red John Comyn met alone in the dimly lighted church, their companions waiting with the horses outside. Comyn had brought an uncle with him, Bruce his brothers. Neither uncle nor brothers were near enough to hear the quarrel, nor to see who struck the first blow. Naturally enough, each faction told a different story.

The Comyn version was that it was premeditated murder. They charged that Bruce lured Red John to the church for that express purpose, and that, even while speaking fair words, he drew his dagger and plunged it into his enemy's heart.

Bruce's kinsmen were positive that their brother had come in a spirit of co-operation, anxious to repeat his offer of his lands and money in exchange for Comyn's support. They swore that Red John had provoked the quarrel and had drawn his dagger first, forcing Robert to defend himself.

Neither side can possibly have had any real knowledge of what actually happened. Of the two men who did know, one lay dead before the high altar, his tongue forever silenced. And Robert Bruce, emerging pale and grim-faced from the shadows, spoke only these brief words, "I doubt I have slain the Comyn."

One man in all the world heard the killer's story, but it was told to him under the seal of the confessional. Bruce did not confess to his friend the worldly Bishop Lamberton, who might have looked with some indulgence upon the removal of a dangerous foe. Instead he sought out the saintly old Bishop of Glasgow.

Bishop Wishart was a patriot, but he was first and above all a priest of the Catholic Church. It is hard to believe that he would have condoned outright murder under the guise of friendship. The fact that Bruce chose such a man as his confessor, and that Wishart of all men granted him instant absolution, would indicate that the fatal blow was struck in self-defense. But all we know for certain is that Bruce killed Comyn at Dumfries, and that Wishart absolved him for it.

Bruce had gone straight to Glasgow after Comyn's death. His brothers accompanied him, and Bishop Lamberton joined him there.

To Glasgow, too, came those Scottish lords who dared risk open defiance of the English king. They were not too many now, for the Comyn-Baliol faction had withdrawn when they heard of the affair at Dumfries. They were a large and powerful clan, and all the hatred they had felt for England now turned upon the Bruces.

Most of the rash young men who had followed Wallace in the early days were dead, or in prison. Moray, Wallace's first friend, had died at Stirling Bridge. Sir William Douglas was a prisoner in the Tower of London, dying of some obscure illness. But there was a Moray present, a bishop. There was also Douglas' son James, a boy of twenty, who was to become Bruce's greatest general.

With good heart the little band of defiant Scots took counsel together. It was decided that their first move should be Bruce's coronation. They could fight, then, not for a hope of their own king but for a king in fact.

Wishing to preserve every form of tradition, they decided to hold the ceremony at Scone, the ancient abbey where Scottish kings had been crowned for four hundred years.

There were difficulties. Edward had carried off the royal robes, along with the crown itself. What sort of coronation could this be, without the customary trappings?

This practical problem was solved by Bruce's sister Christina, Lady Seton. After the death of her first husband, the Earl of Mar, Christina had married an English knight. She promptly converted him into a patriotic Scotsman, ready to risk his money and his head for his adopted land. In the end he lost both.

Most of the men had brought their wives to Glasgow with them. Elizabeth Bruce was there, a quivering, frightened little thing, timidly anxious to be a queen but scarcely able to believe that such good fortune would ever be hers.

It was not the wife but the sister who went among the ladies, demanding their gold rings and bracelets. It was Christina Seton who found a goldsmith and stood over him while he melted the baubles down and formed a skimpy circlet of gold to serve as crown.

Christina next turned her attention to the matter of suitable robes. She persuaded old Bishop Wishart to let her rummage through his vestment-chests, and came up with some very handsome garments. It was actually in the robe of a Catholic bishop that Bruce received his crown.

The company rode up to Scone in the bleak March weather, reaching the old abbey just before Holy Week. The Abbot and the brothers received them joyfully. The ceremony was planned for Palm Sunday, but it was delayed for two days by unexpected news. Isabella, Countess of Buchan, was on her way, and the coronation must be held for her arrival.

The delay for such a cause was more than welcome. The ancient ceremonial of crowning Scotland's king had always been in two parts. One was the seating of the new monarch upon the Stone of Scone. The other, and equally important, tradition demanded that the crown be set in place by the head of the house of Fife. The first Earl of Fife, for loyal service to his king, had asked that privilege, and down the centuries his family had cherished it jealously.

The Stone was in London, and so was the present Earl of Fife, a boy about eight years old. But the little Earl's sister was Isabella, the beautiful young Countess of Buchan. Her husband was a Comyn, closely related to the man who met death at Bruce's hands. Why she chose to volunteer her services as a Fife and crown him King of Scots, we cannot know. She defied her husband to do it, and left home with his curses ringing in her ears.

Matthew of Westminster, an early English historian, says that the reckless Countess was head over heels in love with Bruce, and he with her. This is the only suggestion anywhere of any love affair in his life. His two marriages are noted, with the names of the wives. There is enough authentic material to show the second wife's character, and his indulgent treatment of her. It may well be that lovely brave Isabella held his heart. If she did, he must later have suffered agonies in the knowledge of her fate. The poor lady was to pay dearly enough for her part in the affair at Scone.

On March 29, 1306, Robert Bruce was crowned Robert I, King of Scots. The coronation was a forlorn, makeshift affair, but by all reasonable standards it was a legal one. He was not a usurper, seizing the throne by force, but a qualified heir of the royal house, backed by men of standing in the community.

Those men were few; fewer than twenty in all dared stand openly at his side. Nine of them were to die on the scaffold within the year. Of the others, some fell in battle, and the rest spent long years in prison. Including even the little daughter, not one person who hailed the new king failed to suffer for it in one way or another.

Some shadow of disaster must have fallen over Elizabeth Bruce's spirit as the ladies curtsied before their new queen. She turned pale and fell into a fit of violent trembling. When her husband asked what was wrong, she answered in a voice choked by sobs. "Oh, my lord," she whispered, "it seems to me we are but a May King and Queen, such as the children crown for sport."

It must have seemed to many that the fainthearted Queen had good reason for her fears. Edward of England lost no time when the news of Bruce's coronation

reached him. All the rebel's properties, both in Scotland
and in England, were declared forfeit and bestowed
upon new owners. Bruce's title of Earl of Carrick was
taken away from him and given to the English Lord
Percy.

Thus the new King Robert began his reign landless
and penniless, "a beggar," as Edward gleefully re-
marked. It was as the Beggar King that the English courtiers referred to him thereafter.

Edward himself was growing old, and his health was
failing. He had made a number of expeditions to Scotland in person, always with gratifying results. In the
face of the new threat, however, he found himself
obliged to hand over action to younger, stronger men.
His son Edward, Prince of Wales, was given charge of
the army he raised for the North. In the meantime, he
deposed John of Brittany as Regent and named Bruce's
bitterest enemy Guardian of Scotland.

Aymar de Valence, Earl of Pembroke, was the brother
of Red John Comyn's widow. He was an experienced
soldier, a cold, hard man who had sworn that his sister's
tears would be paid for in blood. He was already in
Scotland, and he acted as soon as the King's command
reached him.

No one knew exactly where Bruce had gone after the
coronation, but it seemed likely that he would be staying

with his good friend Bishop Wishart. Early in June Pembroke attacked the Bishop's castle, Cupar. The guess had been a wrong one, for Bruce and his fighting friends were not there. Only the aged Bishop fell into the Guardian's hands.

The feeble old man, loaded with chains, was sent to England and confined in a stone dungeon. Edward dared not execute him, for he had no power of life and death over a prince of the Church. Wishart lost his eyesight in the dank dark cell, but he lived to be released after Bannockburn.

A few days later Pembroke gathered in Bishop Lamberton and sent him to an English prison. Scouts brought news of Bruce's whereabouts, and the Earl set off in hot pursuit. He came upon the little Bruce army in a wood near Methven.

This, the first battle Bruce fought under his own royal banner, was a disastrous defeat. He himself was taken prisoner on the field but was rescued by his brother-in-law, Christopher Seton. Six of the nobles who had stood beside him at the coronation were captured, Seton among them. Five were to die, and the sixth, Bruce's nephew Thomas Randolph, was to lead an English army against him.

Bruce, with his brother Edward, with his good friends Douglas and the Earl of Athol, rallied such followers as were left to them and made for Athol's estate. There they raised a force of Highlanders and obtained fresh horses. Rested and strengthened, they marched into Aberdeen, where the townspeople were known to be friendly.

As he turned his horse into the inn yard, Bruce was startled by a cry of "Father!" in an excited child's voice. He looked up to see his daughter Marjorie waving at him from an upper window.

He hurried into the inn parlor, to find himself surrounded by weeping women. Queen Elizabeth flung herself into his arms; behind her stood his sisters Christina and Mary. With them were half a dozen ladies, wives of his followers, and a little company of maidservants. The tumult was deafening.

Bruce, one arm around his hysterical wife, raised the other hand commandingly.

"Silence, women!" he thundered. The sobs died to whimpers, and he demanded, "Now, one of you, tell me what this is all about. Christina, lass, your eyes are dry. What has happened?"

"I'm too furious to weep," she answered. "It's a wicked tale, brother, and soon told. King Edward, that noble, chivalrous king, has found a new weapon to harass us poor Scots. We women, Robert, all your kin and those of your followers, are outlawed by royal decree."

"Outlawed?" he echoed.

"You'd like to know what he means by that, perhaps? Well, I can tell you. A copy of the decree was sent to us by a good friend at the English court—I'll name no names, but you recall the business of the spurs. I have the paper here. Shall I read it to you?"

"Read it, girl."

Christina unrolled a parchment and read aloud, her fine eyes snapping. In stately formal language the King of England proclaimed that for all women of the Bruce clan, and of any clans allied with him, the protection of the law was formally withdrawn. "Anyone who chooses," the document stated, "may rob, murder, or violate such women at his pleasure, assured that the law will neither prevent nor penalize him in performing this worthy service to his King."

As the words died, the chorus of sobs broke out again. Bruce gently released himself from his wife's clinging arms.

"There, there, my dear! You're safe now, there's no need for all this distress. Go to your room and bathe your eyes; I'll want to see a smiling face at the supper table. And you others—do you think I came to Aberdeen alone? There are some husbands in the courtyard who will be surprised to see you here. Dry your eyes and welcome your men as good wives should."

Smiling through their tears, the ladies obeyed him. Elizabeth turned docilely toward the stairway. Maid Marjorie ran to catch her father's hand.

"I'm not crying, Father! I think they're silly to cry. I'd rather be here with you than shut up in a stuffy old castle. And Donald didn't cry either."

"Donald?" For the first time Bruce noticed the boy, a year younger than Marjorie, who stood shyly beside her. "Well, bless my soul, it *is* Donald! How are you, lad?"

The young Earl of Mar, Christina's son by her first husband, put a small hand into the great fist outstretched to him. "I'm fine, Uncle. I'm glad to be here with you."

"That's my son!" Christina, who had lingered with the children, gave the boy an affectionate push. "Off with you two, now, and make yourselves tidy for supper."

When they had gone she turned a worried face toward her brother.

"I know we'll be a burden to you, Robert. But what else could we do? That inhuman decree—oh, you can't blame Elizabeth and the others for being frightened! Sometimes I think King Edward is possessed of a devil."

"I've thought the same," he answered soberly. "No, there was nothing else you could do, Christina. We'll manage somehow. Don't worry about it."

"*I'm* not worrying. Like Marjorie and Donald, I can boast that I didn't cry. As a matter of fact, I don't think it's too bad that things have fallen out this way. You and the other men won't be disturbed by anxiety over absent wives. We'll be here, safe under your protection. That should be some comfort to you, surely. I know it will be to Christopher. And that reminds me—he must be wondering why he is the only husband left unwelcomed. I'll go—"

She had been married to Christopher Seton for less than two years. Her lovely face was alight with happiness as she tugged at the old inn door. Pity clouded her brother's eyes as he watched her a moment in silence. Then he laid a gentle hand on her arm.

"Don't go yet, Christy. You need not—that is—well, there's no hurry."

"No hurry? When I haven't seen him since the coronation! That was March, Brother, and it's August now. Don't tease, let me pass. My husband is waiting for me. Robert! You're shaking your head. What do you mean?"

"Christopher is not waiting, Sister," he said slowly. "He did not come with us. He—he will not come. We lost him at Methven, little Christy."

All the light died from her face, but her calm did not break.

"I could not have asked a better death for him," she said steadily. "The first to give his life in your cause, Robert. We must be proud of him."

"We are very proud, my dear. Come, sit here and let me tell you of the battle, and how your Christopher saved my life. I was unhorsed, and captive to an English foot soldier, when Christopher ran the man through and gave me time to mount again. I've seen no braver deed on any field."

"He was always brave. Tell me the rest, Robert. He saved you. And then? I must know how he died. Did you see it done, when they killed my love?"

Bruce took her hand. This was the hardest part.

"Little Christy," he said tenderly, "you must be brave, as he would have you be. Christopher did not die at Methven. They took him prisoner, my dear."

"The English took him?" Stark anguish leaped into her eyes. "Oh, Robert, no—not that! To die in battle, that is a knight's death. But they will kill him as they killed Wallace, torturingly, lingeringly—oh, *no!* I can't bear it, Robert!"

She broke into wild weeping, and with little heart he tried to comfort her. The words he found were hollow, and they both knew it. There was no chance that the captives of Methven would be treated as prisoners of war, eligible for exchange or ransom. Edward had publicly declared that all Scottish rebels were traitors and would meet a traitor's death.

It was months before Christina learned that her tragic forebodings had been justified. With his brother and three good men beside him, Christopher Seton died the horrible death devised for Wallace. For his sorrowing wife, he died on the day that she learned of his capture.

After the first shock passed, she bore the blow with strength and fortitude, more devoted than ever to the cause for which her young husband had given his all. Her broken life was the first Bruce casualty in Robert's struggle. It was not to be the last.

❧ ❧ VII ❧ ❧

THERE WAS NO DENYING that the presence of the women hampered the little company. Word came that Pembroke's army was advancing on Aberdeen, and the Scots took to the hills and the heather once more. They straggled southwestward, making for Kintyre, whose lord the Macdonald offered protection.

It was late summer by now, and the harvest had been poor. Little food was to be had. Queen Elizabeth complained fretfully of the coarse oatcakes that often made their only fare. Young James Douglas, a fine hunter and an expert fisherman, managed to take a red deer once or twice, and sometimes trout and salmon from the mountain streams, but the life was a hard one for gently bred women. Before long it became plain that it was an impossible life.

Sometime toward the end of August they camped on land belonging to John of Lorne. This John Macdougall was a Comyn relative, a very remote one, but that made

73

no difference. All the Comyns were sworn to avenge Red John's death, and they kept cropping up all over Scotland.

Bruce must have known that he was on, or near, the Lorne estate, but he did not know that John had his tenants on the watch. The Bruce camp was taken by surprise, and a sharp fight followed.

This is the battle in which we are told that Bruce slew three brothers, one after the other, with only three strokes of his two-handed sword, "cleaving them from crown to crotch." It must have been quite a feat, but it did not accomplish much. He and his party were glad to get safely away with no serious losses.

When a new camp had been set up in the forest, and supper was cooking on the open fire, Christina came soberly to her brother. Her sister-in-law, the Queen, had taken to her bed of heather in violent hysterics. And while that was of small consequence, the intrepid Christina observed candidly, there was the further fact that little Maid Marjorie had been struck by a spent arrow. Oh, it was only the slightest scratch, no harm had been done. But, next time, could one count on such luck? It was Christina's opinion that an army on the march was no suitable company for women and children.

That had long been Bruce's opinion, too. But what, he asked his sister forlornly, could he do about it?

Christina the resourceful had a plan. There was her first husband's castle, Kildrummie. So far as they knew, it had not yet fallen into English hands. The way to it lay through hostile territory, but if she and her sister-in-law could reach it they ought to be safe. Safer, at least, than they were here in the woods, with the enemy all around them.

Bruce accepted the plan with relief. He gave the women as escort his brother Nigel and the Earl of Athol, with a few fighting men. There in the forest he kissed his weeping wife good-by and promised his little daughter that he would bring her a gay ribbon when he came to her. It was to be eight wearisome years before he saw either of them again.

Nigel Bruce and Lord Athol got their charges safely to Castle Kildrummie, not far from Aberdeen. They had been there for only a few days when news came that the enemy was about to besiege the castle. The fortress was strong and well provisioned. Nigel and Athol decided to try to hold it, but to send the women elsewhere to safety.

Again the Queen and Princess Marjorie took the road with the two Bruce sisters. Somewhere along the way they were joined by Lady Buchan, the fearless daughter of Fife who had placed the crown on Robert's head. Her husband had denounced her as a traitress and was only waiting Edward's permission to hang her from his castle tower. Isabella Buchan was Christina's close friend. Whether the whimpering little Queen welcomed the woman who may have been her husband's sweetheart is unknown, but the party seems to have journeyed along amicably enough.

They made for the convent of St. Duthac. There, by all the rules of sanctuary, they should have been safe. But the Earl of Ross, another Comyn relative, forced the convent door, struck aside the Mother Superior, and carried them off over the protests of the horrified nuns.

The news of the capture was very gratifying to King Edward. With his usual thoroughness, he drew up a schedule of the treatment to be meted out to the prisoners.

Elizabeth was the wife of the man who dared call himself King of Scotland, but she was also daughter to the Irish Earl of Ulster. Edward already had a Scottish war on his hands; he had no desire to stir up trouble among his Irish subjects. Elizabeth was sent to a small country house set in a pleasant park. She was allowed the freedom of the grounds and was given five servants, "the maids to be elderly persons, and not gay." Although she complained bitterly afterward, she was docile enough at the time, giving no trouble to anyone.

It is not likely that her long years of detention distressed her unduly.

Young Princess Marjorie, Bruce's heir, was considered a more important prisoner than her stepmother. She was sent to the Tower of London for a time and later handed over to Henry Percy, the Englishman to whom Edward had given Bruce's earldom of Carrick. Lord Percy also had charge of Marjorie's Aunt Christina and the boy cousin Donald.

For some reason we can only guess at, Christina, the boldest and the most defiant of the Bruce sisters, was treated with comparative leniency, while the full weight of the King's displeasure fell upon her sister Mary.

Mary was a meek little mouselike creature who had certainly been guilty of nothing but having been born a Bruce. Either Edward confused the two sisters in his senile mind or he was making Mary pay for her husband, Neil Campbell, one of the ablest of Bruce's lieutenants. At any rate, Mary was confined in a cage at Roxburgh Castle for three years before she, too, was turned over to Lord Percy.

The details of Mary's captivity are not available. But Lady Buchan's punishment has been described in full in the official English records. Edward's fertile brain devised it, and her husband gave his enthusiastic consent. Like Mary Bruce, she was kept in a cage, this one at Berwick.

The cage was literally that: a latticed wooden structure hung from an outer castle wall, as a bird-cage is hung outdoors. It had a solid roof and floor, but all the outside walls were open to wind and weather, and to the gaze of passers-by. There was room between the wooden bars for rain and snow to beat in; room, too, for a stone to pass, or a handful of mud, or an addled egg. The poor girl—she was not yet out of her twenties—was helpless against these missiles, as she was defenseless against prying eyes and shouted obscenities. She woke and slept, she ate and dressed and bathed, in full view of a curious audience, like some rare animal at the zoo. The audience was always hostile. Decent people, and there must have been many in that sober town of Berwick, hurried past the cage with averted eyes. It was the one poor favor they could do the hapless Countess, to pass her by and not to look.

Lady Buchan endured her infamous confinement for four years. Tradition says she went mad, although the records make no mention of this. At any rate, she was so broken in body, if not in mind, that at the end of the fourth year Edward's successor took pity on her and released her to an English convent. Later she was trans-

ferred to the custody of her husband's nephew, one
Henry de Beaumont.

With the order for this transfer, her name vanishes
from the roll of history. It is assumed that she died
in her nephew's house. When, after Bannockburn, there
was an exchange of prisoners, and all the other captive
women came joyfully home, Isabella Buchan was not
among them.

Thus disappears from human knowledge the brave
and beautiful woman who may have been Bruce's only
love. Even of that we cannot be sure. She threw away
position and wealth, husband and family, liberty, and
finally life itself. For love of the Bruce? For love of
Scotland? The winds of six hundred years have swept
over her unmarked grave, and we shall never know.

Christina's husband, Christopher, was killed in England, as were the other knights taken at Methven. A few
weeks later there was another execution at Westminster,
a very grand one that attracted an unusually large
crowd.

The citizens of that day went to public executions as
we go to parades. Like us, they were highly critical of
the entertainment offered, even though it was free. The
hanging of a common thief would rate at about a neigh-
borhood parade with a school drum-and-bugle corps.

The death of a traitor, and particularly if he happened to be of noble blood, was a major event, well worth taking the day off to watch.

Castle Kildrummie had fallen, and among the prisoners were Nigel Bruce, youngest brother of the Beggar King, and the Earl of Athol. Nigel would have been an important captive, except that his comrade outranked him. Since Edward did not recognize Bruce as a king, his brother Nigel was not considered royal. But the Earl of Athol was a cousin of Edward himself, with the regal Plantagenet blood in his veins. It was not every day that one had a chance to see English royalty die. The mob that swirled around Westminster on that bright October morning were happily confident that this would be a sight worth seeing.

And indeed it was. The Earl of Athol, with due consideration for his rank, had a gibbet thirty feet higher than common, draped in gold-fringed velvet. He was escorted to his doom by the Household Guards in full regalia and ascended the scaffold to a fanfare of trumpets. King Edward was ill at the time, but he was able to watch the spectacle from his bedroom window. Matthew of Westminster notes that this was the pleasantest of the invalid comforts that the great King found to solace his illness.

Nigel Bruce, with two other knights, died at Berwick,

where Lady Buchan hung in her cage. Nigel was just past fourteen, the only Bruce described as handsome. He "made a sweet death, commending his soul to God." The boy was too young to have taken an oath of allegiance to Edward, so he could not have been called a traitor. He was a prisoner of war, taken when Kildrummie Castle fell, and entitled to honorable treatment according to the code of chivalry. Such considerations never weighed with Edward I. Nigel was a Bruce, and for that crime he died in ignominy.

King Robert Bruce knew nothing of these events. All through the autumn he wandered across the countryside, hunted by the vengeful John of Lorne—with bloodhounds, one story tells us—trying desperately to find a resting-place for his little band.

They slept in caves and in thick woods, eating raw oatmeal mixed with brook water when they dared not light a fire. This repulsive mixture, known as drammock or drummock, was the Scots' most effective secret weapon. In days to come, the English, with superior force and armament, were to falter because they had outrun their supply trains. The Scots, fighting on drammock, were never harassed by the ration problem.

After a dangerous and difficult crossing of Loch Lomond, Bruce reached Castle Dunaverty, where Angus Macdonald gave him a warm welcome. John of Lorne was hot on his heels, however, and he dared snatch only a few days of much-needed rest.

He had fewer than a dozen men with him when he slipped away from Dunaverty. His followers had scattered, not in desertion but to return to their own estates for men and horses. Communication was difficult, and the roads were bad, with winter coming on. Winter is a poor time for fighting in the Scottish hills. Bruce and his close friend Douglas decided to seek a safe refuge to await the spring.

They went, by the most reliable account—there is some dispute here—to the little Isle of Rathlin, off the Irish coast. The island belonged to a supporter of Edward, but the lord did not live there, and the Irish inhabitants were sullenly hostile to the English. They offered no aid or comfort to the fleeing Scots, but they did not betray them.

The Scots lived out the bitter winter miserably in a fisherman's hut on the beach. It was in this wretched shelter that the famous spider episode occurred, if it did occur.

The spider story is told, with a great wealth of picturesque detail, by Sir Walter Scott. King Robert, he says, weary and discouraged, debated with himself whether he should continue his struggle for the throne or abandon it completely. Perhaps, Sir Walter imagines his musings, it would be nobler to embark upon a Crusade to recover the Holy Sepulcher, and thus win divine forgiveness for the murder of Red John Comyn. Which was the better goal, Scotland or Palestine?

While his mind wrestled with the problem, his eye was caught by a spider spinning its web on the beam above him. Six times, as he counted, the little creature tried to swing itself across to another beam, and six times the silken thread broke under it.

Bruce, reflecting that he himself had made six futile attempts against the English, took it as an omen. If the spider tried again and succeeded, he promised himself, he, too, would make a seventh attempt. If the insect gave up or failed, then he, too, would give up and embark for the Holy Land.

In the story, of course, the spider succeeded on the seventh try, deciding Scotland's destiny in the act. Scott says: "As he [Bruce] had never before gained a victory, so he never afterwards sustained any considerable or decisive check or defeat."

It is a pretty story, and completely unsubstantiated. If it happened, none of the chroniclers who lived in or near Bruce's time saw fit to mention it.

That does not mean, of course, that it did not happen. Many things happened in that remote day that were not recorded but that have come down to us by word of mouth, stories passed on from father to son. Scott says that the spider story is a tradition of the Bruce family, and that he has never met a Bruce, "or indeed a Scot of any name," who does not believe it without question. Nor, he adds, has he ever met a Scot who would wantonly injure a spider.

The story may very well be true. Bruce was a desperate man fighting for a desperate cause. Other men in like situations have let chance, the toss of a coin or some similar expedient, decide the issue.

The one false note in Scott's tale is Bruce's contrition over the killing of Red John Comyn. He had confessed his sin and received absolution from his spiritual adviser. There is nothing in any word or action of his to show that he ever gave the affair another thought. Scott was writing for his grandson, in the Victorian era when all literature for the young was supposed to point a moral. It is reasonable to conjecture that the good Sir Walter added a few embellishments of his own to his well-told tale.

Whether or not a spider pointed his way, Robert Bruce did leave Rathlin to continue on his chosen path. There, on the bleak wind-swept Irish isle, his fortunes had touched their lowest depths. If he despaired in the fisherman's hut, it was there that he left despair behind him.

Early in February he crossed over to a larger island, Arran. From its shore he could see his lost earldom of Carrick on the southwest Scottish coast. The English Lord Percy was Earl of Carrick now, but Bruce hoped that his people had not forgotten him.

He sent a servant, an old man named Cuthbert, across to Carrick. The man was to find out whether the tenants would rise against their English masters. If things looked favorable, Cuthbert was to light a beacon fire on Turnberry Head, the rocky cliff near the castle.

On a night in March, 1307, Bruce and his friend Douglas saw from Arran's shore a flame blaze up on Turnberry Head. With the few followers who had shared their exile, and with some others they had picked up on Arran, they embarked in small boats for the mainland. In the dark hour before dawn, the King of Scots stepped foot upon Scottish soil again.

❦ ❦ VIII ❦ ❦

As THE ROWBOAT bearing Bruce and Douglas neared the shore, they could see the figure of a man running up and down, waving his arms in wild gestures. Coming nearer, they recognized the servant Cuthbert.

"He's urging us to hurry," Douglas whispered joyously. "How many men has he raised, do you think? If we're strong enough, we can attack the castle at once. Breakfast in your own castle of Turnberry, my King—that will be a fine thing!"

Bruce shook his head. "I can see Cuthbert plainly now. There are no men behind him. Something tells me that we will not breakfast at Turnberry yet awhile, James. Well, we'll soon know!"

The boat grated on the sand, and he sprang ashore. The sleeping castle lay just above them, and Cuthbert spoke in an urgent whisper.

"Go back, my lord, go back! Turn the boats before it is too late! Oh, my lord, I beg of you—go!"

Bruce drew the old man into a rocky hollow at the foot of the cliff. Here, where the breaking waves filled the air with their roaring, they could speak without fear of being heard from the castle.

"Well, Cuthbert?" he said calmly.

"But it is not well, my lord! The Englishman Percy is at the castle, with three hundred men. And——"

"Never mind that," Bruce said impatiently. "What force have you raised for us? You say Percy has three hundred men. How many men have you found for me?"

The servant hung his head. In a low, shamed voice he answered, "Not one, my lord."

"But you lighted the beacon! The signal fire to say that all was well—there it flares on the height. What does this mean?"

Douglas had followed close behind his King. "I know what it means!" he exclaimed. "A traitor among us, lighting the fire to lure us into Percy's hands. You fool! Did you think you'd live to collect the reward, then?"

He drew his sword. The wretched Cuthbert fell on his knees. "My lord Douglas, my lord King—oh, if you will only believe me! I never lighted that fire. It was no work of mine, I swear it. I saw the flames and came here to warn you. I did not set them, nor do I know who did. I think perhaps it was the devil, for everyone knows he fights on the side of the English. Yes, that was it. The devil did it!"

"I have no doubt it was the devil who inspired you," Douglas said angrily. "Well, you can go and tell him how you fared." He lifted his sword, and poor Cuthbert broke into agonized pleading.

Bruce touched his friend's arm. "Wait," he said quietly. He stepped outside the cove and walked along the beach, his keen eyes scanning the heights. When he came back he was smiling a little, without merriment.

"The old man is telling the truth, Douglas. That is no signal fire of wood. It's what we call 'muirburn' in these parts, grassfire. The farmers set it at this time of year, to burn off the dead weeds from their pastures. Not a traitor, and not the devil, but our own folly has betrayed us. I'm a Carrick man; I should have known what those low creeping flames meant. Get up, Cuthbert. No one is blaming you."

Slowly Douglas returned his sword to its sheath. "But this is disaster, Robert. We must get back to Arran before daybreak. I'll tell the men."

"No!" Bruce spoke vehemently. "Here we are in Scotland, and here we will remain. I don't know what we'll do next. But we're not going to turn back now."

"Good man!" Douglas clapped a hand on Bruce's shoulder. "I've had enough of skulking and hiding, myself. What do we do, then, attack the castle? I'm ready."

"Twenty men against three hundred?" Bruce shook his head. "I think not, James. No, we must plan it all very carefully."

James Douglas, always spoiling for a fight, looked a little sulky. "Well, we can't do much planning here," he pointed out. "It's getting lighter already. Soon the castle lookout will be able to see the boats, and—"

"I know, I know." Bruce, his decision taken, moved swiftly. "We must find cover first of all. Come with me."

The last of the boats had landed its passengers now. They waited patiently on the beach, a little knot of devoted men. A few had spent the winter with Bruce on Rathlin; the rest had joined him at Arran. They were shepherds and fishermen for the most part, with a few servants among them. None was a trained soldier, but many had already seen battle, and all knew how to handle the dagger and the spear. They stood in respectful silence as their lord gave his orders.

He hoped it might be possible to keep their landing a secret. They were to pick up the little boats that had served them so well and follow him, keeping as quiet as they could.

Bruce had inherited two major castles, Lochmaben in Annandale and Turnberry in Carrick. Turnberry had been his mother's girlhood home, and her older children had been born there. Although the greater part of Robert's boyhood had been spent in England, his mother had frequently brought her children to Turnberry for long visits. He had waded in the brooks, hunted rabbits in the woods, played robber in the caves.

Sure-footed and certain now, he led his men by unforgotten paths through the heather. He found hiding-places for the cumbersome boats in wild growths of whinbushes, and he brought his followers at last to a secret spot known only to himself and his brothers.

On a desolate hillside a mile from the castle, dotted with boulders and stunted brush, the Bruce boys had once tracked a wounded red fox to its den. The smallest brother was sent into the burrow after the creature and emerged with an incredible tale. The animal, he reported, must be the king of all the foxes. For he lived, not in a mere hole in the ground, but in a fine stone chamber, bigger than the great hall at the castle.

The older boys, though scoffing, were interested enough to dig out the soft earthen sides of the burrow until they could crawl in and see for themselves. The foxes had made their den in a natural cave, an echoing vault lighted by cracks in the rock ceiling. The cracks, masked by bushes on the hillside, gave plenty of air. A little trickling underground stream cut across the far corner.

It had made a fascinating play-place for the Bruce boys. They had turned out the fox family and dragged a great boulder across the entrance. It was their own private secret Robbers' Lair, a safe refuge from grown-ups, an ideal stage for the endless "pretend" dramas of childhood.

Bruce cautiously circled the hill until it lay between him and the castle. The cave entrance was on the far side. Unerringly, among the hundreds of rocks that dotted the slope, he led the way to the right one. With a heave of his mighty shoulders he pushed it aside, revealing the small dark hole behind it.

The earthen passage was a tighter fit now, but he wriggled through it and stood first in the cave. There it was, just as he had seen it last, how many years ago? He was thirty-three now; it must have been a good eighteen years since last he had played robber at Turnberry.

The place had not changed at all. There was the crude fireplace they had made, its stones blackened with the smoke of their cooking fire. The pile of gorse that had made so soft a seat, crumbled now almost to dust. A broken bow that his brother Edward had tried in vain to mend. Discarded toys that must have belonged to the younger boys, Thomas and Alexander. Little Nigel, the baby, had never seen the cave, for he was born after the family's last visit to Turnberry. None of the sisters

had seen it either, he remembered. He and Edward had
cherished the cave particularly as a place to get away
from girls. Poor Christy, how she had pleaded to be
allowed to come once, only once!

"Well, this is perfect!" Douglas's hearty voice broke
in upon his musings. "Light and air—yes, and water,
too. Why, we can hole up here for months, and Lord
Percy none the wiser."

"Let us hope it won't be for months," Bruce answered.
"But at least we can catch our breaths here and think
what is best to be done. First, however—where is Cuthbert?"

The men had squeezed through the opening and now
stood quietly, looking about them in amazement. Old
Cuthbert stepped forward.

"Here I be, Master. But it was the devil lighted that
fire, not me."

"Yes, yes, we know all that. Never mind the fire.
You said you hadn't been able to raise a single man for
us. I can't understand it. It's true the people here
haven't seen much of me since I grew up. But this is
my mother's country; her family have lived here for
generations. Surely there must be men in Carrick who
will take up arms for Lady Marjorie's son?"

The old man shook his head. "Their hearts are with
you, my lord King. But they are humble people; they

dare not cross Lord Percy. That is a cruel man, do you see? He hanged a poacher at the castle gate, and burned down the boy's home so that his poor mother and sisters have no roof over them. And all for one wee rabbit the lad took in a snare! It's not good to cross such a man, that's the truth of it."

"You've talked to them?" Bruce persisted. Half-forgotten names came back to him. "Rob of the Mill— there was a fine strong man! And Angus the Herder, and the smith—Alec, wasn't it? Did you see these men, Cuthbert?"

"I saw them, Master. They wish you well. But they have families, and they are afraid. They won't move."

"Well, if they won't, they won't." Bruce sighed, and looked about him. Daylight was brightening the roof cracks. He called to Douglas.

"Have the men gather some sticks for fuel before full day comes, James," he ordered. "With the the smoke from the muirburn about, we can risk a fire in here. They'd better cut gorse for sleeping, too. We'll be here tonight, and maybe longer."

The men stacked their weapons and dispersed on their various tasks. Soon a fire was blazing in the old cooking place, and the good smell of simmering oat porridge filled the air.

The climb in the raw spring wind had sharpened their

appetites. Bruce and Douglas had eaten their fill, and the other men, too, when the King noticed that Cuthbert was crouching in a corner, muttering to himself.

"Come on, old man, and have your breakfast," Bruce called to him.

Cuthbert shook his head. "I have no stomach for it, Master. This is a bad day for you, I'm thinking."

"And should you go hungry for that?" Bruce laughed. "As you say, it's a bad day for me. But you saw me eat my breakfast just the same."

The old man dragged himself up and came unwillingly to where Bruce sat beside Douglas on a pile of heather.

"I waited till you'd got the good food in you," he said simply. "You'll need your strength to bear what I've got to tell, my lord."

It came out then, all the bad news of the winter, gathered by Cuthbert from the villagers who served Percy's officers. How Castle Kildrummie had fallen, with Athol and young Master Nigel taken prisoner. The story of their shameful deaths, and of the earlier death of Christina's husband and the other prisoners of Methven. She had been right then, poor Christy, when she wept at Aberdeen for the bridegroom she would see no more.

The old man was inclined to linger over the doleful

recital, dwelling in rustic wonder on the splendors of Athol's fine scaffold. With difficulty Bruce hurried him on.

Little Maid Marjorie, then, was locked up in the Tower of London. No, her stepmother was not with her. The Queen had a fine English house to herself, he had heard, with a park to hunt in. The Lady Christina, with her son, was in the English home of Lord Percy—yes, this same Lord Percy who was up at Turnberry Castle now, calling himself the Earl of Carrick. Of Mary Bruce, Lady Campbell, the old man had no knowledge. But he did know, in fearfully minute detail, all that had been done to Isabella Buchan.

With a white face and firm, set lips Bruce listened to all these tales of misfortune. When the old man's quavering voice was still, when Douglas spoke warm words of sympathy, when his men looked at him in awed silence, he spoke only one brief sentence.

"Nevertheless," his strong voice echoed through the rocky cave, "we shall not turn back!"

Bruce and his party remained in the cave for some days, trying to adjust their plans to the changed situation. He had felt confident of Carrick support, and failure to receive it made his position desperate. While he waited, old Cuthbert, their only link with the outside world, brought in more news of disaster.

A Bruce aunt had married a Scot settled in Ireland, Sir Reginald Crawford. The two younger brothers, Alexander and Thomas, had spent the winter in Ireland with their uncle, persuading him to join Robert's cause. Like Bruce, they felt that the best place to strike was in the southern counties, where the family was well known. When Sir Reginald finally consented, the expedition embarked from Ireland and landed in Galloway, next door to Carrick.

They had scarcely stepped ashore when they fell in with Dougal Macdowall, a Comyn man. The details of the fight are obscure, but it ended in the capture of

Alexander and Thomas Bruce, both severely wounded, and their uncle. All three men were sent to Carlisle and hanged there. King Edward was so pleased that he rewarded Macdowall with the hand of a French heiress whose dowry was five thousand hogsheads of Burgundy wine.

Heavy-hearted, Bruce heard of the death of his two brothers. Of the five male Bruces, only he and Edward were left.

His uncle's sons were not likely to support an enterprise which had cost their father his life. The Irish had their own grievances against the English, and they were bitter ones. If Sir Reginald had met with success, it might have led to an alliance between the two subject countries. Well, there was one more hope shattered, that was all.

Bruce was never the man to brood over shattered hopes. He held long discussions with Douglas, and out of them came a crazy plan. It was a plan without a chance in a thousand of success, and it succeeded brilliantly.

Like Bruce, Douglas cherished the conviction that his own people would rally to him if he showed himself among them. He had more basis for this belief than Bruce had had. James Douglas had spent most of his life at Douglas Castle in Lanarkshire. He knew every shepherd, every farmer, by name; he had hunted and fished with their sons, and gobbled oatcakes in their cottages. He simply could not believe that these people would turn a deaf ear to him now.

"I thought the same of Carrick men," Bruce reminded him bitterly. "And you know what happened here."

"But, Robert, it isn't the same," Douglas insisted. "Forgive me, my friend, but this is true. In your early life, you were far more an Englishman than a Scot. You lived in England. When you came to Turnberry, it was only as a summer visitor. You came in English clothes, and I've no doubt the people here thought you gave yourself English airs. Country people notice these things, Robert, and they remember them.

"But I—well, we Douglases have always been stay-at-homes. I was fifteen years old when I went to the English court for the first time, and I can't say I liked it. All that bowing and scraping, and dressing up in velvets and satins—what kind of life is that for a man? I never felt at home there. Give me our Scotch moors, with a good horse under me and the red deer showing its heels ahead—that's the life for a Scotsman. Or for any man. Why—"

"Yes, yes, James." Bruce smiled affectionately at his friend. "I've heard your views on court life before. I won't dispute you. But tell me now, do you seriously think it's possible to rouse Lanarkshire on our side? Remember, your castle is now an English garrison. You should know, better than any man, how strong it is. Your tenants are scattered about on their farms. They have no weapons, if I know the English. I don't question their friendly feelings toward you. But what can they *do?*"

"I don't know. I can only hope that the strong men among them will have the courage to come away with me."

"And leave their wives and children to the vengeance of the English? That's a lot to ask of a man, James."

"It's not too much to ask of a Douglasdale man," James answered obstinately. "Anyway, I can try. Let me go, Robert. This is our only hope."

That was true enough. Desperate though the chance was, it held a faint possibility of success. Bruce himself had failed in a similar undertaking. But if Douglas did not fail—!

Thoughtfully the Beggar King studied the man before him. James Douglas, several years younger than Bruce, was just past his twenty-first birthday. He was dark enough to be known as the "Black Douglas" among his fair-haired kinsmen. Barbour, the Scottish chronicler, says that "he was not so fair that we should speak greatly of his beauty, but when he was blithe he was bonny." Lord James was usually blithe, a cheerful companion who had always a song and a joke for the darkest hour. Men trusted him and followed him, as Bruce well knew. His confidence that his boyhood friends would trust him enough to follow him now might just possibly have some foundation.

"Then go if you will, James," Bruce said quietly. "And God go with you."

They fell to discussing the practical details. Douglas would take only two men with him, he decided, his groom and a young page. They had no horses, of course, so the journey would have to be made on foot. Lanarkshire was not too far from Carrick, and the spring was coming on. Douglas and his two men spoke the Gaelic of the countryside, and could easily pass for farm laborers.

"And don't worry," Douglas laughed. "If the English stop us, I'll have a tale to tell."

"I've no doubt of that. But be careful, Jamie." The King sighed. "I've lost too many good men lately. I can't afford to lose you."

"You won't lose me," Douglas promised. "Don't look for me until you see me, and don't worry about me. When I come, we'll have a feast. Even if not a man will follow me, I won't come back without a shoulder of good Lanarkshire mutton. That I promise you."

Bruce smiled. Good Lord James was extraordinarily fond of good food. More than any of the others, he had chafed at the oatmeal diet of the cave. More than once he had risked all to steal out at night and rob a farmer's henroost or snare a rabbit. In his own county, whatever happened, he would make certain that he ate a few good meals. Of that Bruce was sure.

So, with his King's blessing, James Douglas and his two men slipped away. Once in Douglas country, he went straight to the cottage of his father's old gamekeeper, Thomas Dickson. He was received with tears of joy, and safely hidden. Old Dickson gladly took up the task of sounding out the neighbors.

To the cottage, a lonely one set in the woods, night after night came a stream of men. Dickson had made very sure of their loyalties, and he had chosen well. News of the young lord's hiding place would have been richly rewarded by the English commander at the castle, but Dickson had approached no traitors. One by one they came, stalwart young farmers who knelt at James's feet and vowed to follow wherever he led.

Douglas, gratified by the number of volunteers, was further heartened to find they were not without weapons. As Bruce had feared, the English had demanded the surrender of all arms. But there were knives and short-bows hidden in the thatches of cottages, and many farm tools, axes and pruning hooks and the like, were murderous implements in experienced hands.

Before the week was out, Douglas had raised nearly a hundred men. He might have led them back to Bruce in triumph, but he paused for one exploit that made him famous throughout the land.

A Douglasdale man, who had been called in to repair the castle well, told him that at present there were only thirty soldiers there. The commander, Lord Clifford, was absent with the main force, where or why we do not know.

Douglas questioned the man closely and gained more news of the garrison. The officer in charge, a pious old gentleman, was in the habit of marching all his men to church in the village, leaving the castle undefended on Sunday mornings. This does not seem very intelligent, but it must have been believed that Clifford's earlier activities had completely cowed the population.

Douglas seized the opportunity with glee. On Palm Sunday, as the English soldiers filed into church, they might have noticed that an unusually large number of young male villagers were in attendance.

The congregation knelt and stood for the ritual of the Mass. Just as the priest was chanting his final Amen, the cry of "A Douglas, a Douglas!" rang from outside. It was the signal for action. The Douglas men inside the church sprang to their feet. Palm branches were dropped as knives emerged from under Sunday smocks. Through the open doorway their comrades surged, led by Lord James Douglas himself.

The fight raged fiercely in the church and outside it. The thirty English, taken by surprise, were no match for Douglas and his hundred. Many of them died there in the desecrated sanctuary. Those who survived were marched back to the castle and killed.

The grim stone castle had been left in the charge of two men, a sentry and a cook. The sentry resisted and died at his post. The cook, who had just finished preparing an excellent Palm Sunday dinner, was spared to serve the meal. Douglas and his men sat down and ate it up, and killed the cook afterward.

The castle had been liberally provisioned to stand a long siege. Under Douglas's orders, his men rolled casks of meal, of wheat and salt and wine, into the great hall. All the barrels were broken open, and their contents spilled on the floor. Haunches of venison, crocks of pickled fish, legs of mutton, broken eggs, and vegetables were stirred into the disgusting mess. On top of it all they heaped the corpses of the slain English soldiers. Then, setting fire to the inside walls, carrying off all the weapons and horses they could find, Douglas and his men fled the burning castle.

This is the factual story of the Douglas Larder, a tale of terror with which mothers frightened their babies in days to come. It was planned and carried out by Good Lord James, and it does not seem to have diminished his reputation for goodness in the least.

The sheer ferocity of it is repugnant to modern minds, but Douglas did not live in modern times. He was a man of the early fourteenth century, fighting with such means as came to hand. He knew that he could not hold the castle. When Clifford came back, it would mean death in battle or death on the gallows for the country boys who had chosen to follow him. All he could do, or hope to do, was to give Clifford a sharp jolt, a token that Bruce's friends were still to be reckoned with.

There is no doubt that he made the object lesson as horrible as possible, with deliberate purpose. The English relied on keeping the people quiet by terror. Douglas hoped by the vivid lesson of the Larder to inspire a greater terror. If the people felt that it was not safe to defy the English, they must learn that it was even more dangerous to side with them.

Whatever we may think of Lord James's ethics, there is no questioning his results. Lord Clifford led his army back to a ruined castle, its stone outer walls firm, but the inside a smoking, stinking rubbish heap. The stores that would have fed his men for months were gone,

their quarters uninhabitable. He must have known that
the innocent villagers were laughing behind his back,
and he cannot have failed to remark a dismayed uneasiness among his men.

The story spread, and brought immediate action. As
Douglas and his hundred stole back to the King, they
were joined by new volunteers along the way. Minor
chiefs sought his camp at night, to send encouraging
messages to Bruce. Farmers came in with cartloads of
produce. All through Lanark and Carrick, waverers who
had thought the Bruce cause finished revised their judg-
ments. It is just too bad that all this new surge of support did not come from a nobler source than the hideous
Douglas Larder. But the fact remains that it was the
Larder that did it.

Douglas rode into the Turnberry woods at the head
of three hundred men, all of them armed and many
with horses. He had not forgotten the Lanarkshire mutton he had promised to bring.

Bruce, happy to see him so successful, was confronted
with an immediate problem. It was not possible to hide
so many men, particularly with their horses, in the
Robbers' Lair. The boyhood refuge had served him well,
but its usefulness was past. With Douglas and his following, joined shortly afterward by his brother Edward, King Robert took to the woods again.

Danger lay all about them. Only a mile away, at Turnberry Castle, Lord Percy commanded the coast. Dougal Macdowall, encouraged by the capture of the younger Bruce brothers, was ranging through Galloway, diligently searching for the last of the family.

John of Lorne, a most implacable foe, was at large with his archers and his bloodhounds. Lord Clifford, made ridiculous by the Douglas exploit, was burning to retrieve his reputation. Pembroke, with the main English army of four thousand men, lay somewhere to the south. And just across the Border, in the English town of Carlisle, old King Edward from his sickbed was pouring out a furious stream of command and persuasion, offering fabulous rewards to any man who would bring him the head of the Beggar King.

Fortunately for Bruce, his enemies were operating independently. If there had been any sort of co-operation among them, they could hardly have failed to find him. But each chief wanted the glory of making the capture singlehanded, and none was willing to divide the reward with another. Their lack of unity was the one gleam of light in a situation that otherwise could scarcely have been blacker.

As soon as he left the cave, Bruce split up his following into several smaller bands. Their orders were to

make their way across country as best they could, and
to meet him at a rendezvous in Galloway.

The appointed spot was Glentrool, a wild and lonely
valley near the lake of the same name. Why this particular spot was chosen, and what further plans the
King had, is unknown. An unexpected happening in the
glen was to change all plans and make Glentrool immortal. A monument stands there now, to mark the site
of King Robert's first victory.

❦ ❦ X ❦ ❦

BRUCE made his own way toward Glentrool through the crisp spring weather, accompanied only by one or two men. According to some versions, he traveled entirely alone, disguised as a monk or a beggar, depending upon the teller. This particular section of his wanderings is so tangled in fact and fable that it is impossible to speak about it with assurance.

Douglas, who burned his castle on Palm Sunday, can scarcely have reached the cave before the first of April. The battle of Glentrool was fought sometime before May 1. Robert's journey to Glentrool, therefore, cannot have occupied more than four weeks at most. Yet into those four weeks the old chroniclers have crowded no fewer than twenty-three incidents, all giving glowing testimony to Bruce's extraordinary prowess.

The stories are colorful and exciting, and they show their hero as something larger than human. They range from an adventure with Lorne's bloodhounds, the ferocious beasts cowed into fawning servility by Bruce's fearless eye, to an affair at a ford, where he slew two hundred men alone and singlehanded. There is a charming account of his arriving late at a cottage door, asking for shelter as a homeless wayfarer. The goodwife answered that all homeless men were welcome in her house, for the sake of one homeless wanderer who would soon rule the land. Bruce is said to have disclosed himself as the wanderer she meant, and to have enlisted her three sons on the spot.

It is probable that all, or most, of these are "cherry tree" stories, the myths that inevitably grow up about the name of a great man. It is worth pointing out, however, that such tales are invented only when the man is great enough to carry them. Bruce was brave enough to fight two hundred men, humble enough to seek shelter with the humble. If the stories themselves add nothing to our historical knowledge, they do throw a revealing light on the character of the man who inspired them.

Whatever adventures befell him on the way, Bruce came, in late April, to the meeting place in the glen. Edward Bruce and Douglas were already there, with about one hundred and fifty men. The other bands had not reached the rendezvous.

In one way or another, the Earl of Pembroke heard that Bruce was in Glentrool. Such rumors were coming into his camp every day. Bruce had been seen here, he had been seen there, he was most certainly to be found in such and such a place. The Earl had run down all the rumors and found them false, and he was beginning to be a little skeptical. There can be no doubt that some of the cautious Scottish countrymen, not yet willing to take up arms for Bruce, delighted to show their sympathy by deliberately confusing the English commander.

Pembroke, taking no great stock in the Glentrool story, could not afford to ignore it. He chose a woman spy, a harmless-appearing old soul who wandered about the valley gathering herbs.

One of Bruce's sentries, hidden in a thicket, watched her through the long afternoon. Something about her actions aroused his suspicions. At sundown, just as Bruce and his friends were sitting down to supper, he marched her into camp.

She was stumbling along at the point of a spear, weeping and howling for mercy. The soldier prodded her forward.

"A prisoner, my lord," he said proudly.

The woman's wails grew louder, and Bruce frowned.

"Nonsense, man. What sort of prisoner is this? A weeping old woman! Here, Mother. Stop that racket. We're not going to hurt you."

"She's a spy, sir," the sentry insisted. "I could tell

by her actions. Sent here by Pembroke, I've no doubt. If we let her go, she'll run back and tell him where to find us."

Bruce laughed. "I doubt if her joints were made for running, lad. She looks worn and spent to me. Yes, and hungry, too. Goodwife, will you join us at supper? Of course you will. Douglas, you were always one to wait on the ladies. Help our guest to the rabbit stew."

The old woman crouched on the ground, devouring the good hot food. Bruce and Douglas continued their talk, paying no attention to her, and the sentry sulkily returned to his post.

Twilight had fallen by the time the meal was finished. The camp went early to bed, for a gleam of light carried far on these hills, and all fires had to be extinguished before dark.

Bruce, like everyone else, slept on a bed of grass beneath the open sky. As he rose from the stone on which he had been sitting, the old woman stirred and mumbled at his feet.

"Our prisoner—I had quite forgotten her." He bent over the dark heap. "Asleep, it seems. Well, let her be. It's too late for her to find her way home tonight."

"I suppose she *isn't* a spy?" Douglas said doubtfully. "After all, such things could be. The English aren't far away, Robert. If Pembroke heard we were here—"

"If Pembroke heard that, he'd be here himself, with his army behind him. No, Douglas, this is just some poor lone creature gathering simples; you can see them any day in these hills. Let her rest. And—wait a minute. I've a plaid here I won't be needing." He whipped the Highland cloak off his shoulders and carefully tucked it around the sleeping woman. "The dew falls chill on old bones. Well, let's be off to bed."

The soldier cook, rising to prepare the breakfast porridge, found the pot already boiling on a newly kindled fire. The broad stone that formed the officers' table was neatly laid, and beside Bruce's place lay a little twisted nosegay of rosemary and bog-myrtle.

Bruce picked it up and sniffed it as he sat down. The old woman, helping him to porridge, explained, "For luck, your lordship. Wear it beneath your jerkin, and the enemy's sword can never pierce your heart."

Gravely the King thrust the bunch of leaves inside his jacket. "Thank you, Mother. You wish me well, then? You don't want to see my enemy reach my heart?"

The old woman straightened and set down the porridge pot.

"When I came here," she said slowly, "I did not know what manner of heart you had, my lord. They told me you were an evil man. They said you wanted to bring ruin and death to our land. They said it would be a service to the King to find where you hid, so that the English might punish you. I am an ignorant woman, my lord. I believed them."

Douglas gave an exclamation. "Then she *is* a spy! Robert, we must—"

"Wait. She has more to say, I think. Go on, Mother."

The old woman's eyes strayed to where Bruce's cloak, neatly folded, hung on a near-by branch.

"I have only this to say, sir. That they lied to me. They told me your heart was bad, and I have found that it is good. I do not serve those who hunt down a good man. I will serve you if you will have me, my lord. I am a woman and old. But I can cook; I can wash your shirts. Let me stay here with you."

Without answering her, Bruce drew Douglas and Edward aside. For several minutes the three leaders talked in excited whispers. Then Bruce beckoned the old woman to him.

"You have offered to serve me, Mother. I take you at your word. There is a service you can do me, one that no one else can perform. Look up there. Do you see the crag above us?"

The old woman raised her dim eyes. "Craigmin, my lord. I know it well. Many a time, in my young days, I have climbed the rocky path they call the Steps of Trool.

Now it is too steep for my old legs. What would you have me do, Master?"

"An easy task, goodwife. Go back to the Earl of Pembroke. Tell him you have found the Bruce. Offer to guide him to the spot. Then lead him here, to the foot of the Steps of Trool, and scuttle home again. Will you do this for me?"

"I had hoped to stay with you," she said slowly.

"I know. But if you can help me by going back, you will not refuse?"

"I'll not refuse." She sighed, and gathered up her bundle. Already Bruce's men were striking camp, loading their few possessions on their backs.

"Don't go too fast," he warned her. "Give us the day to prepare. Then at nightfall seek out the Earl and tell him the tale. When he is ready, lead him across the glen. You need not choose the easiest road," he added.

The old woman cackled. "Be sure I would think of that. But I don't understand this, my lord. You are asking me to betray you. Surely that can't be right?"

"It's entirely right," he assured her. "Only make certain that you don't linger in the glen when the Steps are reached. If the English offer you a reward, try to get them to pay you before you start, or you will never collect it. As for myself—well, the King of Scots is a beggar, as everyone knows. If I had gold to give—"

"I'd not take gold from you!" the old wife answered swiftly. "Let the English pay, as they will. But if I could have the horn spoon from which your lordship ate his porridge, I'd be a proud and happy woman."

Smiling, he gave her the spoon. She took it, and knelt to kiss his hand. Then, wagging her head in bewilderment at the ways of the gentry, she made off down the glen.

To this day, a lofty ledge on the face of Craigmin is pointed out as the King's Seat. From it, next morning, Bruce and Douglas watched fifteen hundred English soldiers ride into Glentrool, the old herb-gatherer leading the way.

The glen, a valley between precipitous mountains, is not a level plain but a series of sharp rocky slopes leading steadily upward. The heavy English cavalry horses slipped and stumbled over the stones, and progress was almost impossible. Sir Geoffrey de Moubray, the English commander Pembroke had chosen, finally ordered his men to dismount, and sent the horses back.

On foot, the English archers followed their guide, who led them up and down hill, choosing the roughest spots. They were already footsore and weary when they followed a narrow shore path along the lake and came out at the foot of the Steps of Trool.

The old woman pointed. "Up there," she croaked.

Sir Geoffrey frowned. "Are we goats, to climb that crag? Surely there must be an easier way."

She shook her head. "No other way, your lordship. But once past the crag, the going is easy. There is a little plain, and a wood beyond. Then another clearing, and another wood. It is in the second wood that the Bruce lies, all unsuspecting. When you have climbed the crag, a half-hour's gentle march will bring you to him."

"Well, all right," the commander grumbled. "Lead on, then."

The Steps, a natural giant's stairway of rock, were so narrow that only one man could scramble up at a time. The old woman climbed up a step or two, then squeezed herself against the rock wall to let an impatient soldier pass her. She stood there, panting in a great show of exhaustion, as the vanguard went by. No one noticed when she slipped back to level ground and melted into the bushes. She was well on her way home when the King's bugle sounded on the heights above.

With the notes of the horn came a shower of arrows and the thunder of falling stones. From the stunted oaks and pines and huge rocks that crowned the Steps, the Bruce men rained death upon the invaders, strung out in a long line on the stairway and along the shore. Many were toppled into the lake and drowned; many more were crushed by the great rocks that came hurtling down.

The English bowmen could not see their targets on the cliff above them, and their great number only made for greater confusion. Before an hour had passed, Sir Geoffrey was fleeing in ignominious rout.

The battle of Glentrool was the turning point in the war for Scottish independence. It was the first victory in what was to become a long series of victories. There was yet a great way to go, but the Beggar King had taken the first step that was to lead him into his kingdom.

❦ ❦ XI ❦ ❦

THE EARL OF PEMBROKE received the news of Glentrool with a fury that threw him into an attack of apoplexy. Although he tried hard, he was unable to keep his King in ignorance of what had happened. Edward, still gravely ill at Carlisle across the Border, sent him a sharp warning that he would retrieve the distaster or hand over his sword.

Pembroke relieved his feelings a bit by degrading the unlucky Sir Geoffrey in rank, and set out at the head of his army.

Bruce, of course, had not lingered in the glen. He moved back into Douglas country, showing himself boldly in the open this time. As he passed through Carrick he was joined by volunteers from his own lost estate, the very men who had refused to join him at Turnberry. From Carrick and Douglasdale he collected enough recruits to bring his fighting strength up to six hundred men. Pembroke had about three thousand when the two armies met at Loudon Hill.

Again Bruce was able to choose a battleground to his liking. He knew that Pembroke was advancing along the highroad that led inland from the important town of Ayr. One stretch of the road ran along the side of a small hill covered with peat moss, a soggy growth that makes impossible footing for horses.

Here, as at Glentrool, Bruce showed his peculiar genius for winning battles against overwhelming odds. He knew this Scottish land from his long wanderings, and he had imagination enough to make the land fight for him. Such failures as he was to have from now on were in the hazards of conventional warfare, where castles were to be stormed or battles fought on the open plain. Under such circumstances, he was still vulnerable to English arms and numbers. He was never to be defeated when he could utilize the terrain to his advantage.

The highroad from Ayr was on solid ground, with peat moss on either hand. Bruce dug three trenches across it, leaving a narrow hard passage in the center, the only path that Pembroke's cavalry could follow. Bruce and his best men were in the first trench as the English approached, and the second and third trenches were filled with pikemen.

The trenches were Pembroke's undoing. The arrows of his bowmen overshot the ditches in which the Scots crouched. Out of the trenches a hedge of pikes thrust upward, piercing the bellies of the plunging horses. The maddened animals swerved into the peat-bog at either side, and Bruce's men burst out of the ground to finish their riders with sword and spear.

Pembroke's vanguard was annihilated. He, with his main army in reserve, did not attempt to make good the initial disaster. He turned about and rode back to a safe castle in Ayr, there to await in shuddering anticipation his royal master's newest outburst.

Edward of England was so furious that he forgot his illness. Sick or well, he himself was apparently the only man strong enough to put these rebel Scots in their proper place. He rose from his bed and called for his horse. To his courtiers it was a miracle that this tottering wreck, wasted to a skeleton by long illness, could climb into the saddle.

Nevertheless, at the head of a mighty army, Edward I set out on his last invasion of Scotland. At Burgh-on-Sands, within sight of the rebellious land, his short-lived strength failed him. He died in the castle there. With his last breath he committed to his son the carrying out of the enterprise to which he had given eleven years of scheming and fighting. Young Edward, Prince of Wales, solemnly promised his dying father that his sword would not be sheathed until Scotland was conquered.

The old King's body was carried back to England,

where it rests in Westminster Abbey. Prince Edward, who was to have married the Maid of Norway and become King of Scots the easy way, would have need of a powerful sword indeed to hew his path to that coveted throne. He was not, in any sense of the word, the man for the job.

King Edward II of England, as he now became, was twenty-three years old when his father died. He had none of his father's force of character, and very little of his ability. His first act was to discharge every adviser the older man had favored and to surround himself with personal friends. Pembroke, who had been the old King's regent for Scotland, was deposed, and the office given to John of Brittany, who had held it before. The unhappy Earl, who had expected to lose his head over the Loudon Hill defeat, must have felt that he got off very lightly.

Young Edward, having buried his father with a great show of mourning, lost no time in arranging matters to suit himself. The counselors he chose were young men, good fellows, at home in the hunting field and the banquet hall. There was nothing vicious about the new king. He liked drinking and gambling and dancing, but his dissipations were moderate for a young man in his position. His best trait was his unswerving loyalty to his friends; his worst was his innate weakness of character, which made him an easy prey to unscrupulous men. Good-looking, affectionate, easygoing, and kind, he should have made an admirable ruler. But he trusted where he should not trust, bringing such misery upon his people that when he came to his pitiable end there was not a man alive who pitied him.

His father's death gave Edward his first opportunity to enjoy life in his own way. He was engaged to a French princess whom the older Edward had chosen for him, a masterful young woman of little charm. He suspected—rightly, as it proved—that when she became his wife she would frown upon his playboy activities. Into the summer after his father's death, his last summer of bachelorhood, he managed to crowd as many amusements as his imagination could suggest.

The new King's best friend and drinking companion was a young French knight from Gascony, one Piers Gaveston. Edward I had distrusted the Gascon's influence so much that he had banished him from England. The young King called him back and made him Earl of Cornwall, a huge estate with rich revenues.

In no time at all, this seedy adventurer had the simple-hearted Edward completely under his thumb. Gaveston was utterly without principle, his only purpose the advancement of his own interests. He played shrewdly upon Edward's dislike for the older men who had been

his father's friends, lampooning them with a merciless
wit that brought tears of laughter to the King's eyes. It
might have been wiser if Gaveston had been less amus-
ing at the barons' expense. But the dashing, debonair
Frenchman, intrepid gambler, superb dancer, and delightful storyteller, had considerably more wit than wisdom. He was a companion exactly after Edward's own
heart, and with impudent assurance he assumed leadership of the younger set surrounding the King. Edward's
last bachelor summer was the gayest one the English
court had known for many years, or was soon to know
again.

Robert Bruce, learning of the older Edward's death,
naturally expected that the invasion would proceed without him. He was relieved as well as surprised when the
son turned around and led the army back to England,
on the pretext of escorting the body to Westminster.

It was not until August that the new King, mindful
of his father's dying admonition, returned to Scotland.
He did not get far, and he did not stay long, although
no one opposed him.

He traveled in state at the head of the army, but the
expedition was organized as a sort of protracted picnic.
With Gaveston and other boon companions he visited a
few castles safely held by the English, put their cus-
todians to considerable expense for food and wine, and

looked for rebels where none were to be found. Since he could not find them, he cheerfully assumed that they did not exist. After a few pleasant weeks, he went home again for a final round of pleasure before he sailed to claim his French bride.

For the summer at least Bruce was free of an English invasion. His successes at Glentrool and Loudon Hill had brought him new support. For the first time his claim to the throne began to have a real possibility of success.

All over the country, where Scots had resigned themselves to English domination, the old national pride stirred into new life. Many were cautious of giving it expression, for all the strong castles were still in English hands. But Bruce's exploits had kindled a flame, and the horizon showed a brightening glow.

This would all have been very heartening, except for one thing. Scotland was not a united country. Now that it began to seem possible that she could throw off the English yoke and be governed by a Scot again, the old vexatious question arose. Which Scot? If the land was to have a native king, who would that king be?

Bruce and his friends were in no doubt. Scotland already had a Scottish king, Robert I, legally descended from the old royal house and properly crowned at Scone Abbey. All that his countrymen had to do was to enlist under his banner and by united effort to drive the English out.

So indeed it should have been. The land would have been spared an extra year of blood and tears, of devastation and bitter suffering, if his fellow-Scots had accepted Bruce's leadership in 1307. Many of them did. But the old question of the disputed succession was not yet settled. The Baliols were a powerful clan, and their claim seemed as good as it had ever been. If Scotland was to have a king, they argued, then that king must certainly be John of Baliol, whom Edward I had enthroned and then deposed.

Former King Empty Jacket was living peacefully in France with his son. No one troubled to ask him whether he wanted to return to the turbulent life of Scotland. His relatives, the Comyns and the Buchans, simply assumed that he or his son would welcome restoration. The two families had personal grudges against Bruce: the Comyns the killing of Red John, and Lord Buchan his wife's part in the coronation. The breathing space afforded by the English withdrawal had scarcely begun when they took up arms against Bruce.

So it happened that the Bruce had a civil war on his hands, with his English war not yet won. For the next year his military genius had to be directed not against the common enemy but against his own countrymen.

It was a sorrowful business, and he hated it. Time after time he appealed to the Baliol faction, for the sake of the motherland they both loved, to give up this senseless strife between brothers. His pleadings were useless, and the succession war was fought out to the bitter end.

❦ ❦ XII ❦ ❦

BRUCE, after leaving his winter refuge in the Isle of Rathlin, had spent the spring and summer of 1307 in Carrick, Galloway, and Lanarkshire, all counties in southwestern Scotland. In the late autumn he received word that the county of Moray, in the north, was arming to support his cause. His friends there had taken Inverness Castle, and were urging him to come and rally his northern well-wishers to further effort.

Bruce reached Moray in October. The English forces there were commanded by the Earl of Ross, a Scotsman, but a Baliol man. Lord Ross was the general who had captured Bruce's womenfolk at St. Duthac convent. He was a religious man, and his conscience had bothered him ever since. His priest had rebuked him sharply for his invasion of the convent and his discourtesy to the nuns. In addition, there was remorse for the terrible fate to which he had betrayed the courageous Lady Buchan.

His remorse, and the further fact that he was an

honest and honorable man at heart, with a deep love of country, no doubt influenced the negotiations into which he entered with Bruce. The official excuse was that winter was coming on, and a winter campaign in that rigorous climate was almost impossible. Whatever his reasons, Ross willingly agreed to a truce until spring, giving his word not to attack Bruce or interfere with his movements.

This peaceable arrangement neutralized the north and left Bruce free to deal with his two most violent enemies, John of Lorne and the Earl of Buchan. The Lorne territory lay south and west; Buchan's ancestral land was to the east of Moray. Bruce, rather than wait for his two enemies to close in upon him, boldly decided upon an expedition against Buchan.

The first snow of the year was already falling when he reached Inverurie, a small town dangerously close to Buchan. There disaster overtook him. He fell dangerously ill of "a chill and a fever," probably pneumonia.

Inverurie, a mere cluster of herdsmen's huts, had little comfort to offer a sick man. His comrades sheltered him in a wretched cottage whose chinks let in the icy wind; they made his bed on a pile of cloaks. His army doctor, with the best of intentions, weakened him by bleeding and by a diet of thin gruel. The expedition against Buchan came to an inevitable halt while he lay there, a little nearer to death each day. In the stirring events of the next few weeks, the Bruce has no part. The Earl of Douglas, Good Lord James, was making history on his own.

When he had moved north, Bruce had left Douglas with a good-sized force in the south. Lord James, a stubborn man, had never reconciled himself to the idea that the English should possess his own ancestral castle.

He had held Douglas Castle for a few hours on the memorable occasion of the Larder. He had done his best to ruin it, hoping that if it could not be his it would at least offer no safe shelter to the English. But the fire he set had not harmed the solid stone of the outer walls, and the enemy had replaced the burned woodwork inside. Its present governor was an English knight named Sir John de Wanton.

Sir John, "ane gud bachelor," was young and brave, and he was in love. The lady of his choice, quite in the manner of fairy-tale princesses, had set him a task. Since the Larder episode, Douglas Castle was a fearsome place, and Douglas himself a dreaded menace. The people of the countryside, fearing his displeasure, were unwilling to supply food and fodder to the castle. The post of governor of Douglasdale had gone begging since Clifford's departure, with no English knight anxious to take it up.

Sir John's lady love, desiring to test both his devotion and his courage, had promised to marry him on condition that he rule Douglas Castle for a year and a day. He had come from England, young and eager, and established himself in the gloomy keep. His year had seven months to run when Douglas reappeared in his home county.

Lord James had two hundred tough fighting men with him, but he knew the castle's strength too well to try taking it by direct assault. Instead, he devised one of those stratagems in which his quick mind delighted.

Learning from the villagers that the castle was desperately short of hay, he told off fourteen men to gather great bundles of it, throwing it across their saddles. He disposed the rest of his men in a little wood near the castle, well hidden among the bushes. The fourteen, with countrymen's smocks pulled over their armor, were sent to lead their hay-laden horses past the castle gate.

The result was exactly as Douglas had hoped. The English sentry, seeing fourteen farmers on their way to market with a fine stock of hay, reported it to his commander. De Wanton ran to the battlements, shouting to them to stop and bargain. The "farmers," as though frightened, turned their animals around and made off toward the wood.

The lovesick Sir John, who had seen little action in

his dreary Scottish sojourn, immediately called for his horse and with a strong bodyguard set off in pursuit. At the edge of the woods, the supposed countrymen tore off their smocks, flung the hay to the ground, and leaped into their saddles. The rash young knight found himself confronting a small body of well-armed cavalry.

He rode at them gallantly enough, his men clattering behind him. But the ambush was well planned. They were out of sight from the castle, and Douglas sprang from the bushes with an overwhelming force. Poor Sir John was cut down early in the fighting. On his body they found a letter from his love, reaffirming her promise.

His garrison surrendered the castle without a struggle. This time Douglas took no chances. He spared the lives of the English soldiers, but he set them to work taking the castle apart. When they had finished, not one stone remained upon another. Douglas Castle was a shapeless heap of rubble, never again to harbor Lord James's enemies.

Douglas sent off a messenger to report the triumph to his King. But Bruce lay wasted and delirious on his pile of cloaks, and it was his brother, Edward Bruce, who sent back congratulations and orders to remain in the south.

The elder brother's illness had thrown the whole

weight of such decisions upon Edward's shoulders. He had followed faithfully in Robert's shadow, not so brilliant a soldier as Douglas, but brave and reckless. Now that there were grave doubts whether Robert would ever recover, Edward began to entertain ambitions that had never before entered his head.

The legitimate heir in the event of Robert's death was little Maid Marjorie, his only child. But the Maid was a captive, she was very young, and a girl. Edward, cautiously talking things over with the men around the forlorn Inverurie camp, found many to tell him that a male Bruce of fighting years would have a better chance at the throne. It is not certain whether the idea originated with them, or with him. But from Inverurie on, Edward Bruce never quite lost the hope that he might wear a crown.

The facts about Bruce's illness were so well guarded that the news did not reach Lord Buchan until early December. As soon as he heard it he moved toward Inverurie, setting up his camp three miles away at Old Meldrum. From there, at daybreak on Christmas Eve, he attacked Bruce's quarters.

The story runs that the sick king, hearing Buchan's bagpipes skirl out the war song of an enemy clan, sprang from his bed and compelled two men to hoist him into the saddle, sitting fore and aft to hold him there.

It is possible, of course, but highly unlikely. In any

event, it was not Robert but Edward Bruce who met the attack with such vigor that Buchan's forces broke and ran. It was Edward Bruce who chased the fleeing Earl for twelve miles, to the safe refuge of Fyvie Castle.

It was Edward, also, who carried out the series of raids into enemy territory that became known as the Herschip (laying waste) of Buchan. In the first three months of 1308 he overran Buchan's lands, firing granaries, driving off cattle, burning villages, and leaving desolation behind him.

The Earl was not particularly popular with his tenants, and Edward's campaign against their homes made them sullen and restive. Many of them deserted to the Bruces. In the end, Buchan left his home county with such followers as remained to him and went to Galloway, where he joined forces with John of Lorne, and with the Macdowall who had murdered Bruce's younger brothers.

Sometime during the months the Herschip raged, King Robert Bruce surprised his doctor by making a complete recovery. This happy event, we are told, was hailed with tears of joy by all about him. Whether Brother Edward's tears were all for joy we cannot know. But whatever disappointment he may have felt, he hid it stoically and without murmur resumed his role of second fiddle to his distinguished brother.

Robert, when his strength came back, found himself

with an army that had grown amazingly after Edward's raids. He led it toward Aberdeen, where the citizens declared for him. Aberdeen Castle, with its English garrison, held out for a few weeks but was finally taken.

He moved on through the northeast, and by summer's end in 1308 he had captured the castles of Fyvie, Kintore, and Aboyne. Following the example of Douglas, he destroyed the castles as they came into his hands.

England's writers have indignantly condemned the "barbarousness" of this policy, which blotted some fine old buildings from the Scottish landscape. The fact is, however, that Bruce's "barbarousness" was sound military strategy.

The castles were strong forts from which the possessor could dominate the countryside. They would have been of great value to Bruce, if he could have been sure of keeping them. But he did not have men to spare for garrisons, or provisions to stock them. His own forces could operate very well in the open, profiting by their familiarity with hill and wood, and the friendliness of the people. The English were at a disadvantage with no strong points in a hostile countryside. Bruce, destroying the castles, left the foreigners "no hole to lurk in" and forced them into the war of movement in which he excelled.

The truce with the Earl of Ross had been extended,

so that the middle north remained neutral. With Buchan withdrawn to the south, with the northeast solidly behind him, Bruce was able to turn his full strength against John of Lorne.

He took his time, making his preparations with thoroughgoing care. To strengthen his expedition he sent for Douglas. Good Lord James arrived, flushed with recent successes in the south. He brought an unexpected prisoner with him.

❦ ❦ XIII ❦ ❦

DOUGLAS, riding north at the head of his men, found his King comfortably lodged in a monastery near Old Meldrum. The Scottish clergy, inflamed by the treatment of Bishops Lamberton and Wishart, were fiercely pro-Bruce. After the death of Comyn, Edward I had induced an English Bishop to pronounce a sentence of excommunication upon the killer, declaring Bruce no longer a son of the Church. This sentence the Scottish churchmen had flatly refused to recognize, even when later it was confirmed from Rome. So far as we have any evidence, Bruce continued to worship in whatever parish he found himself and was never once refused the rites of his religion. Churches and abbeys opened their doors to him and his followers, generously donating food and money at a time when both were sorely needed.

Douglas' arrival, although expected, had been delayed by the spring rains. It was late when he rode up to the abbey door. The porter brother received him cordially.

"Our lord the King is sleeping," he explained, "but he left orders that he was to be roused if you came, whatever the hour. If you will come this way, sir?"

Douglas slid down from his horse. "We have ridden far today. My men are weary, and hungry, too. Can you see to them?"

The porter bowed. "Their billets are waiting, my lord. Reverend Father had us prepare the stables with bedding and food for the men, and provender for the horses. I will attend to them as soon as I have shown you to the King's chamber."

"Good. Lead on, then." He turned to a young man who had also dismounted, and who stood silently beside him.

The boy—he was not quite nineteen—wore no armor and carried no weapons. His hip-length quilted jacket, of the sort commonly worn under chain mail, was rust-marked and torn. A bloodstained bandage bound his forehead.

"Come with me, Thomas," Douglas said sharply. "The King is waiting for us."

The boy's chin went up. "His Majesty the King is in England. There are no kings here."

Douglas's jaw set. Without a word he seized the boy by the arm and hurried down the passage after the porter. The monk paused at a door and knocked.

"Who's there?" called a sleepy voice.

"The Earl of Douglas, your Grace. You said for me to bring him to you when he came."

"Of course, of course. Come in, James. This is good news!"

The porter opened the door and lighted a candle from the lantern he carried. Bruce was sitting up in bed, pulling a loose woolen robe about his bare shoulders. Douglas hurried to him, and Robert clasped him in a warm embrace. The porter withdrew, and the prisoner stood sullenly inside the door.

When the first greetings were over, Robert asked, "Who is the prisoner you've brought me, James? You were very mysterious about it. An enemy commander, but not an Englishman, you said. And one that I know well. Don't keep me guessing. Who is he?"

The flickering candlelight scarcely touched the pale-faced boy at the door. Douglas beckoned to him. "Come here, lad, and greet your King!"

Reluctantly he came forward. When he reached the bed where Bruce sat, he bowed stiffly.

"I greet my lord uncle. I see no king."

"Thomas Randolph!" Bruce sprang up and seized his nephew's hand. "Oh, but it's good seeing you! We haven't met since the battle of Methven, when the English took you prisoner. Tell me, what happened to you?

And how did you escape? Your comrades, the two
Setons and three others—we heard of their shameful
deaths, but of you there was no word. You were so
young, only sixteen, Thomas. That was why they spared
you? Because of your youth?"

"No!" Young Randolph's voice rang out defiantly. "It
was not my youth. It was my loyalty that won me the
King's grace!"

"Your loyalty—to Edward of England?" Robert
asked quietly. "I thought you had sworn loyalty to me,
Thomas."

Randolph flushed. "I was a child; I knew no better.
After I was taken prisoner, they showed me what a fool
I had been. The Bishop of Durham himself talked to me.
He made me see you as you are, Uncle, a rebel and a
murderer, an outcast from our Holy Church. Oh, you
can't deny it! Not only did you take up arms against
our lord the King, but in the cloister at Dumfries, before
the very high altar itself, you murdered Red John
Comyn. And for that sin the Church has cast you out.
How could I follow a heretic the Church itself has rejected?"

"Well, better men than you are doing it!" Douglas
put in angrily. "Robert, I'm sorry about this. I shouldn't
have inflicted this young idiot on you. But I hoped that

you could make him see reason. Heaven knows I've tried, but—"

Bruce waved him to silence. "Just let me get the situation clear, James. Thomas is your prisoner. An enemy commander, you said. Then he was in arms against us? I didn't know. I think you'd better tell me the whole story."

Angrily, Douglas poured it out. One of his men had offered to guide him to an empty house near the Water of Lyne where he could set up headquarters for his southern raids. They approached the house late at night, and to their surprise they saw light shining from its windows. Stealing closer, they found that it was occupied by a body of English horsemen who were scouring the woods for rebels. Their commander was Sir Thomas Randolph. Douglas had surrounded the house and taken him prisoner with his men.

"I should have hanged him, as the Macdowall did your brothers," he concluded furiously. "But it's not too late. I hoped the sight of you would bring him to his senses. A foolish hope! Well, I'll send him to the stables under guard for the night. Tomorrow—"

Young Randolph did not flinch. "Hang me, by all means," he said coolly. "It is what one would expect when one deals with murderers."

Bruce's calm eyes surveyed the two men before him.

"Let me be sure I understand, Thomas. You were captured at Methven, along with your Aunt Christina's husband and four others. They were executed, but your life
was spared. Was that on condition that you take up arms
against me?"

The boy shook his head. "There were no conditions.
After my eyes were opened, when I understood the sort
of man you are, of my own free will I offered my sword
to England. If I have helped, in any small measure, to
bring our unhappy land of Scotland back to peace and
order, I shall go gladly to your scaffold!"

Douglas snorted, but Bruce asked mildly, "Then you
love Scotland, Thomas? You acted, not through hope of
winning English favor, but for your country's sake?"

For the first time the boy's hard young face quivered.

"I am a Scot, Uncle. Do you think I don't love my
country? Ever since I can remember, we've been torn by
quarrels and strife. There's no happiness in the land,
and there can't be, so long as this goes on. England—
what do I care for England? But only England is strong
enough to put an end to this wretched squabbling among
ourselves. Once the King's mighty arm has restored
peace, we can be happy again."

Bruce sighed. "I hadn't thought of it before. It's true,
Thomas, that in your short lifetime we've had no peace
in Scotland. Think of it, Douglas, a whole generation has

known nothing but war and desolation! No wonder our youth is bewildered and resentful."

"That's neither here nor there," Lord James answered bluntly. "We'd all like peace, young Thomas. Yes, and we'll have it. But not at the price of bending our necks in slavery to England!" He gave an exasperated laugh. "Why I waste words on him I don't know. I've argued with him all the way up from the south, Robert, and you can see how little I've convinced him. Well, maybe the hangman's rope will prove more eloquent."

Thomas shot him a defiant glance but remained silent. For a moment there was no sound in the little stone chamber. Then Bruce spoke, his voice soft with a quiet gentleness.

"I remember you as a baby, Tommy, a little red-headed Bruce in my sister's arms. She was so proud of you! Long dead now, poor girl. But I don't think we'll hang her son, Tommy."

"Hang me if you wish!" The boy's voice cracked. "I'm not asking mercy from *you*."

"And I am not offering mercy." Bruce's calm face grew suddenly stern. "You are a prisoner, Thomas Randolph, taken in battle by Lord James Douglas. As his superior officer, it is my business to pass judgment upon you. Listen well to what I say, for you must abide by it."

"You can hang me," the boy repeated obstinately.

"I've told you that you will not hang! This is your sentence. This is what you must do."

He paused for a moment, and then went on, "We are resting here at Meldrum while we prepare a summer campaign against John of Lorne. His chief ally is Dougal Macdowall, who sent your uncles Thomas and Alexander to their death. Do you remember your Uncle Alec, Thomas? Once he carried you pickaback across a fen, and you called him Uncle Horse. Well, no matter. As I say, we shall be here for several weeks. While we remain at this place, you will serve as the esquire of Lord James. Oh, yes, I know I made you a knight before Methven! But now you are a simple esquire again. You will polish his armor for Lord James, prepare his bed, serve him at table, see that the groom attends properly to his horse. Do you understand?"

"I hear you," Thomas muttered.

"Very well. See that you obey those orders. Call the sentry, James, and have him sent to your quarters. And then come back, old friend. I want to talk to you. Goodnight, Nephew."

Thomas turned on his heel without reply and followed Douglas outside. Lord James did not look too well pleased when he returned alone.

"You've done me no favor, saddling me with that

young wildcat," he growled. "I'd like to know your reason."

Bruce laughed. "A little experiment, my friend. If it doesn't work, he can take his place as an ordinary prisoner of war. But it's worth trying. Sit down now, and make yourself comfortable. There should be a bottle of wine somewhere hereabouts."

He fumbled in the rushes that strewed the floor and brought up a bottle. "The good Abbot put it there against the chill of the night, he told me. Yes, here are horn cups, too. Well, your health, James!"

"And yours, Robert!"

Relaxed and at ease, the two men drank and chatted of Douglas's adventures in the south. Presently, however, James came back to the question of Randolph.

"I still don't understand what you're trying to do, Robert. What's the good of making him my esquire? It's certainly no good to me, I know that."

"But it ought to be good for him," Bruce answered. "James, when you captured Thomas there at the house on Lyne Water—he put up a fight, didn't he?"

"Oh, yes, he fought like a cornered wolf, I'll say that for him. Powerful shoulders he has on him, and he handles the claymore like a veteran. If the fellows with him had been as good, I might have a different story to tell."

"I thought as much. He's got Bruce blood in him—

yes, and the Randolphs are fighters, too. You wouldn't say the boy lacks courage or skill, would you, James?"

"I'd never say that. But he fights on the wrong side."

"I know. And at his age, and past it, I was fighting on that side too, my friend. Have you forgotten?"

"Well, you don't encourage us to remind you," Douglas said candidly. "And after all, you soon saw the light."

"And I think young Thomas will see it. I think we can show it to him, James. Remember the terms of his sentence. He will be constantly at your elbow. The English got at him with fine talk. All right, we'll let him hear our talk. They set their priests to make me out a black heretic, cast off by the Church. Well, let him find out that Bishop Durham's ban does not run in Scotland—no, not even though they badgered the Holy Father into confirming it! Thomas will see that his heretic uncle goes to Mass on Sunday like any Christian, and that the sacrament is not denied him. That will open his eyes!"

"But the young fool is so obstinate," Douglas protested. "Do you think I haven't explained all that? I talked myself black in the face, and he won't listen."

"Talking won't do it, James. But maybe seeing will. Let him see with his own eyes, hear with his own ears. The boy is not stupid, and he loves his country. I think we can make something of him. At least, for the sake of my dead sister, I'm going to try."

Skeptically enough Douglas agreed to the experiment. Its success more than justified Bruce's hopes.

Thomas Randolph, with a natural military talent as great as Douglas's own, stood respectfully silent behind his knight's chair while campaigns were mapped. He served at table when Bruce entertained visiting chiefs, hearing the wrongs of English rule. He could not fail to see the respect and affection with which Scottish church-men served their King.

Little by little his sullen resentment melted as he came to a clearer understanding of his uncle's character and aims. He was shy of Bruce, but the day came when he haltingly offered to Douglas a useful suggestion for dealing with John of Lorne.

When the expedition got under way, at the beginning of summer, Thomas Randolph marched with it, a captain commanding a troop of Moray volunteers. He was to become Douglas's closest friend, and his ardent rival in daring feats of arms.

Long years later, with death soon to snatch the hard-won scepter from him, Bruce confided his kingdom to Thomas Randolph, Earl of Moray. As regent for Bruce's son, the child-King David II, Randolph continued until his own death the free Scottish rule that his valor had done so much to establish.

❦ ❦ XIV ❦ ❦

ALEXANDER MACDOUGALL OF ARGYLL was the great-uncle of Red John Comyn, and like every other male relative of Comyn he had sworn to have Bruce's life. Alexander himself was nearly a hundred years old, so that the burden of revenge fell upon his son, John of Lorne.

John had come perilously close to capturing Bruce in the early days of his wanderings. He could count upon the solid support of Macdougalls and Macdowalls, all Comyn relatives and all eager to help crush the upstart king.

John's estates of Lorne and Argyll lay on the west coast of Scotland, midway between the country's northern and southern boundaries. He was master of a "navy," a hundred galleys propelled by manpower. The oarsmen were old men and boys, not considered first-rate fighting material but very skilled at maneuvering the small craft in coastal waters. Along the rugged coast

147

where roads were few, John was able to transport his men by water, landing them wherever he chose. This gave him an advantage not shared by the inland chiefs.

All through the summer of 1308, the clans gathered at John's castle of Dunstaffnage, streaming in from island and mountain, every chief bringing his following of armed men. Buchan lay ill in Galloway, and was to die before the year ended. Except for him, practically all of Bruce's bitterest enemies among his own country-men were gathered at Dunstaffnage Castle.

There were no Englishmen at John's side, and few English sympathizers. The battle, when it came, would not be fought on behalf of Edward of England. It would be a struggle between Scot and Scot, a bitter grudge fight on the Comyn side, a life or death business for Bruce. If the King won, the Comyn-Baliol faction would be effectively crushed. If he lost, it might well be that he would lose all hope of the crown.

With so much at stake, Bruce chose to stage the inevi-table clash on Lorne's own ground. He was in the mid-lands, where prudence might have dictated that he wait for the enemy to come to him. Instead, with Edward Bruce and Douglas as his chief aides, he marched boldly into Lorne.

He had about eight hundred men, not more than forty of them mounted. Two hundred were archers; the others were armed with battle-axes and pikes. Bruce and his officers carried the claymore, the fearful two-handed sword, four feet long and capable of splitting a man in half. Every man had a dagger at his belt, and knew how to use it in hand-to-hand fighting. They also knew how to make effective use of the natural weapons with which the rocky soil of Lorne would provide them.

They left the midland towns behind them and marched west into wild, mountainous country, almost uninhabited. It was a land of desolate moorland and brawling torrents, studded by long narrow lakes or "lochs," overgrown with brushwood, strewn with immense boulders. The only roads were sheep tracks, the only habitation an occasional shepherd's hut.

It was rough going for an army on the march, but Bruce's men managed it without difficulty. Most of them were Highlanders, well accustomed to such terrain, and at home in it. They scrambled nimbly over the stony slopes, slept beneath the summer stars, and ate their oatcakes with good appetite.

When he came to Loch Awe, at the foot of towering Ben Cruachan, Bruce learned that he was within a few miles of the enemy. Lorne had left his castle and come out to meet the invader. The scouts who brought the news did not know exactly where the Lorne forces lay, but they warned the King that he had "a great multitude" with him, all of them thirsting for vengeance.

Bruce left his men in camp for the night and stole out to reconnoiter, taking only Douglas with him. The two friends had often stalked deer together in country like this. Not a footstep sounded, not a twig snapped to betray them as they crept forward to the point where Loch Awe turns into the River Awe and rushes into the larger Loch Etive.

Ben Cruachan, highest of Scottish mountains, rises in a steep cliff here, with a narrow path at its foot, along the riverside. On the far side of the river rise lesser cliffs. Bruce's men, if they advanced, would have to follow the road beside the river, called the Pass of Brander. There was no other way.

With the steep mountain on one side, and the foaming torrent on the other, Brander Pass would be a perfect spot for an ambush. Sure that he would have chosen it had he been in Lorne's place, Bruce did not underestimate his enemy. A touch on Douglas's arm, and the two men left the path to worm themselves painfully and silently up the mountainside.

Lorne was a strict disciplinarian. The men he had posted on the lower slope of Ben Cruachan showed no lights; there was no sound of voices. But the keen eyes of Bruce caught a gleam of starlight reflected back from armor; there was a chink of metal on stone as a man shifted his cramped limbs under a thornbush. The friends did not climb far. There was no need. As silently as they had come they stole back into their camp beside the lake.

Bruce gave an order, and the sleeping men roused themselves. Douglas went among them, quickly choosing the hardiest and the quickest witted. He lined them up before the King, who explained the mission on which Douglas would lead them.

They were to climb Ben Cruachan, quietly and in the dark, to a point above that chosen by Lorne's men. There they would lie in wait, while the main army advanced along the road. Then, when Lorne's ambush discovered itself, they were to act.

"In other words, you will ambush the ambushers," he explained. "Is that clear? Very well. You will leave your armor behind, for its weight would hamper the climb. Take only your bows slung behind you—we don't want the scrape of pike on stone to betray us. And, above all, be silent! Remember, the lives of all of us are in your hands."

They stood before him, a band of stalwart, rawboned Highlanders, quietly nodding their understanding of the task he had set them. Without their armor, they looked the farmers and fishermen they were. The tartan had not yet reached the popularity it was soon to attain, and most of them wore natural-colored linen smocks. But there was a sprinkling of plaid cloaks in varying patterns to mark the clans, and many of the younger men had adopted the free-swinging tartan kilt. Bruce himself was to popularize the national dress as a point of Scottish pride, but that day had not yet come.

With Douglas leading the way, the ambush party set off long before dawn. Up they went, clutching at whin-bushes and clumps of grass, noiseless and speedy, skillfully by-passing Lorne's men on the lower slope.

Bruce broke camp at daylight. He marched his division cautiously into the Pass of Brander, and was not surprised when a shower of arrows suddenly rained upon them from the mountainside.

Even as Lorne's men went into action, a great boulder rolled down upon them from above, followed by more stones and arrows. Bruce left the path and led his men upward, so that the Lorne men were caught between two fires. They broke and ran for the pass, pouring along it with Bruce in hot pursuit.

He chased them to the point where the River Awe empties into Loch Etive, a fair-sized lake with an outlet to the sea. It was on Etive that Lorne had stationed his fleet of galleys, which he commanded in person. He had sent his main force into the pass, where they tangled with their fleeing comrades from the hillside. In the confusion, many were pushed off the path and drowned in the rushing water.

John of Lorne had an excellent view of the melee from his flagship. He was by no means a coward, and whatever plan of battle he had made must have included good use of the ships. Whatever that plan was, Bruce had upset it. Lorne turned his galley about and made off for Dunstaffnage Castle, at the mouth of Loch Etive.

Bruce rested for a few days, counted his prisoners, among whom he found some of his bitterest enemies, and then moved on to take Dunstaffnage Castle.

With the bulk of his army gone, John of Lorne put up only a perfunctory defense. His old father surrendered, and John with his fleet slipped away to the Western Isles. From there he went to England and mortgaged all his English possessions to pay his father's ransom. He served King Edward until his death, but he was never again to menace the Bruce.

The victory at Brander Pass was supremely important, for it eliminated the coalition of Scottish chiefs who opposed Bruce's rule. It was important also for another reason, and a highly practical one. It gave the hard-pressed King his first opportunity to make some money.

For years Bruce had been literally penniless. His income had come from his Scottish and English estates, now confiscated and given to others. Douglas and the other chiefs who supported him were in the same situation. It was impossible to pay the fighting men, or even to arm or feed them.

Fortunately swords and battle-axes do not wear out, and it is possible for a bowman to make his own arrows. For food there were always the country people, who would give it if they felt generous, or exchange it for work done if they did not. Many a time the Bruce army halted to bring in some farmer's hay or help in the shearing, their only reward the night's meal. It was a beggar army, led by a beggar king, that crushed the Lorne might below Ben Cruachan.

With that victory, however, everything changed. Many noble prisoners turned up among the captives, rich men whose families would pay well for their release. Bruce drove some hard bargains before he set them free.

This was not, as some might think, a characteristic example of Scottish thrift. The ransom was an honorable feature of war up to that time and for centuries later, its origin lost in antiquity. Shakespeare quotes Antony as saying of Caesar, "He hath brought many captives home to Rome, whose ransoms do the common coffers fill." Bruce was following a long established precedent when he set a price on his prisoners' heads.

He was also acting in strict accord with custom when he seized everything of value in the castles that fell to him. It was not to his credit or discredit, but merely a piece of extraordinary good luck, that he captured so many wealthy prisoners at Brander Pass and that Dunstaffnage Castle was richly furnished.

The monetary gain, of course, was a very minor one compared to the political triumph the victory afforded. Lorne had been thorough in his canvass of Bruce's enemies, uniting almost all of the powerful ones under his banner. His defeat was the defeat of the whole concerted movement. Individual animosities were to smolder for a long time, and after Bruce's death the Baliols were again to throw the land into turmoil. But while Robert I lived, he never again had to face serious opposition from the Comyn-Baliol faction.

Shortly after Dunstaffnage was taken, the Earl of Ross surrendered the north without a battle. This meant that Bruce was now undisputed master of the northern half of Scotland, including the Buchan and Lorne lands.

In the more thickly settled half, south of the River Tay, there were still strong castles in English hands, and great chiefs whose sympathies were with England. Ross's surrender had ended the civil war, in which Scotsmen fought each other for the throne of Scotland. But Bruce had still another and greater war on his hands. He had still to wrest his throne from the powerful English.

He knew that immense difficulties lay ahead of him,

but it was with a lighter heart that he turned back to the English war. Robert Bruce had never relished the shedding of Scottish blood. It saddened him to face as foes such men as John of Lorne, whose courage and ability would have been valuable in restoring the devastated kingdom.

Whenever it was possible, he won his late opponents to his side, treating them afterward with the same generous friendliness that he gave his own supporters. Many of them joined him, among them the Earl of Ross, who later married his youngest sister Maude. Ross, a skilled administrator, rendered valuable service in setting up law courts and civil services when peace finally came.

Bruce had need of all the friends he could muster now. If only the Scottish scene is considered, the year 1308 had been one of unbroken success. After Ross's surrender, Robert summoned a Parliament and took the first steps in establishing a functioning government. But far away to the south the English Parliament still made laws for Scotland, and an English king had not renounced his authority as Lord Paramount.

❧ ❧ XV ❧ ❧

THE YEAR 1308, a lucky year for Bruce, brought nothing but misery to Edward II of England.

The young King had not had an easy time of it while his father lived. He had been dragged off on Crusades, "sorely bit by the fleas of Palestine," and forced to live the hard life of a soldier in the field. He had supposed that, now he himself was King, he could have a little comfort and some innocent fun. His wife and his barons soon undeceived him.

The new French wife, Isabelle of Guienne, was only fourteen years old, but she was a woman of iron. She had no beauty, no kindliness, and no sense of humor. She took a violent dislike to Edward's close friend, Piers Gaveston, whom she accused of laughing at her. Gaveston's brilliant wit was his chief charm in Edward's eyes, but to Isabelle it was a deliberate offense.

From the first, the French bride showed an inflexible determination to be the master of the house. As the modern historian Hume puts it, "Finding that her husband's capacity required, as his temper inclined him, to be governed, she thought herself best entitled, on every account, to perform the office." She had scarcely landed in England before she set herself to displace Gaveston and establish her own authority over the weak-willed King.

Poor Edward, a man born to be bossed, found himself surrounded by bosses. Gaveston, gay and tactful, exercised his dominance so pleasantly that the young King thoroughly enjoyed it. Isabelle's shrewish rule was bad, but when he looked outside the home he found even harsher masters.

His father's friends, the older nobles he had dismissed from the inner circle, were not long in divining his weakness. They came together under the powerful Earl of Lancaster, and formed an alliance against him.

All of them had seats in Parliament. Without difficulty they rushed through a law banishing Gaveston from the kingdom. For good measure, the bishops among them threatened excommunication for the unpopular favorite if he remained in England.

Edward I, in the improbable event that his barons had dared take such action against him, would have clapped them into the Tower and chopped off their heads. His unhappy son wept bitterly and began to think of a good place to send Gaveston that would not be out of visiting distance.

He appointed his friend Lord Lieutenant of Ireland, conferring new lands and riches upon him. This would have worked out beautifully, except that his imperious wife promptly forbade him to visit Ireland, even for short visits.

The King wept some more and refused to eat his meals. Isabelle could not let him starve himself to death, because as yet she had no child. If there had been a baby prince for whom she could act as regent, she said callously, "my lord might please himself in the matter of sustenance."

As it was, she reluctantly went to the barons and pleaded that Gaveston be allowed to return, on condition that he conduct himself "with a decent humility." Isabelle and the barons were on excellent terms, united in hatred for Gaveston and contempt for Edward. They yielded to her request and grudgingly consented to Gaveston's return. All they asked in exchange was that the King turn over the government to twelve of their number, a committee which would have all the powers vested in the crown.

Edward, who had never found his governmental duties anything but a bore, thought this was a very cheap price to pay for the joy of regaining Gaveston's company. He left Westminster, where Parliament sat, and established himself at York. Gaveston joined him there. In hunting and jousting, drinking and gambling, getting up amateur dramatic productions, and playing practical jokes, the two young men passed their time as of old. Queen Isabelle sulked and raged, but her tantrums could not dim Edward's delight at being reunited with his favorite.

From this time onward it was the great nobles of England, and not her King, who carried on the war against Scotland. The committee later relinquished its powers, restoring them to Edward, but he was never anything but a puppet ruler. Believing in his right to govern Scotland, and mindful of his father's dying wishes, he responded willingly enough when the barons prodded him into action. But there is little doubt that if they had left it to him he would have made peace years before peace finally came.

The English barons were divided among themselves on the Scottish question. Some of them were for continuing the war; others were in favor of seeking a settlement. The peace-lovers were strong enough, early in 1309, to send an envoy to Bruce, asking on what terms he would discontinue hostilities.

The messenger they chose was Bruce's old friend Bishop Lamberton, released from prison for the purpose. They let the Bishop out on parole, requiring him to post a bond of six thousand marks for his return.

Edward's treasury was the richer by that sum, for Lamberton did not go back. He sent a messenger saying that his mission had been unsuccessful, since he could not find the person to whom Edward's letter was addressed. Edward, or the barons for him, had written to Bruce as the Earl of Carrick, his former title. Bruce and Lamberton realized, before the letter was opened, that it contained no recognition of his royal rank, and therefore of Scottish sovereignty. Until that recognition came, it was useless to talk of peace.

Peace talk continued, however, all through the early part of 1309. Bruce had established friendly relations with King Philip of France, who urged the English to make a settlement with him.

Philip's efforts procured the dispatch of another emissary to Scotland. This time it was the Irish Earl of Ulster, Bruce's father-in-law. Bruce received the old gentleman affectionately, and was pleased to learn from him that Elizabeth was in good health and spirits. But when he was offered another Carrick letter, he again refused to read it. Ulster went back, with a Scottish guard of honor to the frontier, and reported that the Scots were stronger than had been supposed and would never compromise until their end was gained.

By midsummer of 1309, the war party among the barons was in the ascendancy. Queen Isabelle, taunting her husband with cowardice, helped the young King to make up his mind. He gathered his army and moved on Scotland, taking Gaveston with him as chief of staff. It must have been a relief that the Queen stayed at home.

The army, supported by forty-two ships following along the coast, was large and unwieldy. Edward reached Berwick in September and from there crossed into Scotland.

The country was in the grip of the severest drought it had ever known. No rain had fallen since early spring, and the grass was tinder-dry. Under Bruce's orders, it had been set afire, so that Edward marched through scorched, dead fields, in search of an enemy who never showed himself. Great rocks and fallen trees had been rolled across the roads, and bridges cut. The English King wandered about for several fruitless weeks and then went back to Berwick, where he dug in for the winter. Several of his ships were captured or sunk by Scottish privateers under the command of Neil Campbell, Mary Bruce's husband.

Campbell, a splendid sailor and a keen fighter, had assembled a little fleet of galleys and fishing vessels. In December he used it to attack the Isle of Man, in the Irish Sea. The attack was a feint, designed to draw out the English fleet. Edward's captains obliged him by hurrying to the waters around Man, where Campbell engaged them so effectively that several ships were sunk. Still more were captured and added to the growing Scots navy.

Neil Campbell and his ships were to play an important part in coming events. Since Scotland is bounded on three sides by navigable waters, he was often able to supply beleaguered garrisons that could not be reached overland. The English also depended on sea-borne supplies for their coastal strong points, and Campbell was in position to cut them off.

Most of the year 1309 and the two years that followed it passed in a sort of stalemate. Edward kept his army immobilized at Berwick, sending occasional raiding parties north. The most effective of these was led by Gaveston, who had some temporary success at Perth. Edward tried hard to build up his friend as a military hero on the strength of it, but no one paid much attention.

The barons, who had been all for pushing the Scottish war, were inclined to let Edward get on with it while they ran England to suit themselves. Occasionally they summoned the King home to sign some decree, and sometimes they scolded him for not having any Scottish victories to report. But for the most part they let him alone. He and Gaveston were happy enough at Berwick, where they set the army engineers to laying out a race-track.

Bruce had summoned all his strength to prepare for a massive English invasion. He was agreeably surprised when nothing happened. He had a little time to organize his disorganized country.

An assembly of bishops, held at Dundee in 1310, formally recognized him as King of Scotland, sending a statement to that effect to the Pope. This unanimous support of the Church strengthened his position abroad. France, Norway, and Flanders accredited ambassadors to his court. Except in the view of England and of English-minded Scots, Robert I was now King in fact as well as in name.

He knew, of course, that in spite of all this encouragement Scottish independence did not yet exist. It could never exist while mighty England claimed overlordship. The English still had, and would always have, superior resources of men and money and war matériel. A large-scale expedition into the enemy country would have been suicide. Nevertheless, he did what he could.

At intervals during the quiet years he sent his brother over the English border, in a series of lightning raids that struck terror into the countryside. Edward Bruce burned villages and carried off grain and cattle, food

badly needed by the Scots, who were still feeling the
effects of the recent famine.

The English district of Northumbria, sadly harassed
by the raids, offered to pay two thousand pounds for
a truce. This businesslike arrangement was later made
with a number of towns in northern England, and
worked out to the general satisfaction. The English villagers were free of worry, and the Bruce war chest benefited.

While the clouds appeared to be breaking for Bruce,
they were thickening fast about King Edward's unlucky
head. The nobles to whom he had handed over power
were treating him with increasing contempt. With the
birth of her son in 1312, Queen Isabelle threw off all
pretense of wifely loyalty and openly joined his enemies. It was largely due to the Queen's spite that the
old question of Piers Gaveston was opened again. She
protested to the barons that the Gascon was not, as he
had promised, conducting himself with a decent humility.

Edward and Gaveston received a peremptory summons at Berwick. They were to appear at once before
Parliament, and show cause why Gaveston should not
return to exile.

Edward hurried back, but he did not take Gaveston
with him. The favorite was dropped on the way at
Scarborough Castle, a supposedly impregnable for-

tress. The King went on alone to plead for his friend.

He found all the great nobles of England arrayed against him. Besides his cousin and enemy the Earl of Lancaster, there were Lord Pembroke, who had commanded the first Edward's army in Scotland, the Earls of Warwick, Hereford, Arundel, and many others. They told Edward flatly that he must get rid of Gaveston for good.

These men who dared give orders to their King were not rebels. They were all members of Parliament, not elected, but holding office by virtue of their rank, as members of the House of Lords still do. The Magna Charta granted by King John a hundred years before had ended absolute monarchy in England.

The power of Parliament, in early days, was as strong as the reigning king allowed it to be. Edward I had put up with no nonsense. Any rash noble who felt inclined to stir up trouble in Parliament was likely to find himself accused as a traitor, or a heretic, or a trafficker in black magic. Any of these charges, before a judge of Edward's appointing, was certain to bring a guilty verdict and a sentence of death. The vacant estate and title could then be conferred on a new man who would have sense enough to see things as the king saw them.

Poor henpecked Edward II was not the man for such

strong measures. In a quavering voice he begged the barons not to tear his beloved companion from him, vowing that he could not live without Gaveston. Lancaster answered shortly that there would be no objection if Edward chose to abdicate and accompany his friend into exile.

It might have been a wise choice, but Edward was incapable of making such a decision on his own initiative. He dithered about, and finally started off for Scarborough to see what Gaveston thought of the idea. But his enemies got there before him.

Lord Pembroke besieged Scarborough Castle, where Gaveston made a poor defense and surrendered on the third day. They carried him off to Warwick, and murdered him there.

Shock and grief threw the young King into an illness that lasted for several weeks. When he recovered, Lord Lancaster waited upon him, very humble and penitent. He and his friends, he said, realized that they had gone too far. Honestly feeling that Gaveston's influence was bad for England, they had let their patriotic fervor sweep them into committing a crime. They urged him, as soon as his strength permitted, to attend a ceremony they were arranging in Westminster Abbey. Then, and only then, could their royal master realize the depth of their contrition.

The ceremony, held the following Sunday, was quite a spectacle. Twelve of England's haughtiest lords, dressed in sackcloth, crept up the Abbey steps on their knees. When Mass was over, they knelt at the altar and publicly confessed their mortal sin, asking pardon of God and of their King. The Bishop of London, speaking for Heaven, graciously granted them forgiveness. Poor bewildered Edward, with his sharp-tongued wife at his elbow, could do no less.

There followed a short-lived era of good feeling, during which Edward and his barons were on excellent terms. Even Isabelle forebore to nag him. He was very fond and proud of his infant son, another Edward. Fatherhood seems to have stiffened his backbone, while it turned his thoughts back to his own father. He remembered, as Piers Gaveston had made him forget, that there were other things in life besides having a good time. He had promised his dying father to subdue Scotland. Six years had passed, and the vow was not yet fulfilled.

Friends again with the lords, sobered by grief, and determined to give his new-born son a greater heritage, Edward II once more began gathering a mighty army for the invasion of Scotland.

❧ ❧ XVI ❧ ❧

EDWARD'S preparations for renewing the war were elaborate, and they took a great deal of time. England had no national army. Every noble had a certain number of armed retainers and could supplement it by calling up the able-bodied men on his estate. The common man served his lord, bound to him by oath, as his lord was bound to the king. When summoned to do so, he took up arms and fought under his lord's leadership. The cause in which he fought was no business of his. The lords, in turn, were subject to call by the king. The resulting army was made up of men from all parts of the country, each under his own leader, with the king in supreme command. When the fighting ended, the army quickly broke up as the men returned to their peace-time occupations.

For the mighty thrust that was now in preparation, months of preliminary effort were required. Armor and swords had to be forged by the slow handicraft of skilled workmen. There was the need to build ships, another process that could not be hastened. A huge amount of time, labor, and money went into the building of the siege-train, pride of Edward's heart.

The siege-engines that made up the vaunted train were the last word in modern warfare as the early fourteenth century knew it. Gunpowder had not yet come into use, so that the nearest thing to explosives was the so-called Greek Fire. This was a highly inflammable combination of sulphur and niter with many uses. A piece of tow dipped into it and tied to an arrow could start a fire at a considerable distance. Most well-designed castles had pots for Greek Fire set about the ramparts, ready to ladle out flame to besiegers below. Its use in burning wooden bridges and enemy stores was invaluable.

Edward's siege-train included horse-drawn carts specially built to carry vats of sulphur and of niter separately, for the mixture had to be made as required. There were many more wagons, however, laden with weapons even more terror-inspiring than the Greek Fire. Some of them, mounted on what we should recognize as crude gun carriages, were giant catapults capable of hurling good-sized stones. There were scaling-ladders and battering-rams. But strangest of all were the siege-gibbets.

A gibbet was a skeleton wooden tower, used in peacetime executions of prominent criminals. It was not the same thing as a gallows, although the words are often used interchangeably. The gallows was simply a crosspiece supported by two posts, and to be hanged on one carried no social distinction whatever.

Every English village had its gallows on the green, and there were hundreds of them all over London. Any common pickpocket could meet death on them. But the gibbets were specially built for the occasion, and such honors were reserved for the gentry. To be hanged on a gibbet you had to be at least the younger son of a knight, although for that lowly rank you could not expect much elevation from the ground. The higher the rank the higher the gibbet, as we saw in the case of the King's cousin Athol, who met his death more than thirty feet in air. He had velvet draperies on his gibbet, too, but that was a refinement only attainable to those of royal blood.

While any handy man could knock a gallows together, gibbet-building was a skilled trade. For his siege-train, Edward called in all the expert gibbeteers of the kingdom. The task he had for them demanded quite a bit of engineering knowledge. He wanted gibbets, and bigger and better gibbets than had ever been seen before. He wanted them to be demountable—perhaps prefabricated is the better word. At any rate, they were to be cut and sawed to fit, sturdy enough to bear extremely heavy weights, and thoroughly tested. Then they were to be taken apart for transport by wagon or ship.

Edward's super-gibbets were not intended for hanging purposes, although they would be handy in case he captured any Bruces with their noble blood. But the gibbets were intended for the mounting of catapults and Greek Fire pots, and the scaling of castle walls.

Some of them, when his workmen had done their best, were as high as any castle. They were a real and ingenious threat against the stone castle-forts of Scotland. They would undoubtedly have proved their worth in the war against Bruce, except for one thing. By the time Edward and his gibbets arrived, there were no castles to besiege.

In building his siege-train, as in most of his actions, Edward showed his incapacity to learn from experience. Although most of the Scottish nobles were now on Bruce's side, the castles that had been theirs were still garrisoned by English soldiers, commanded either by Englishmen or by Scots who were friends to England. Their doors would open to Edward willingly, with no need of siege.

Even poor foolish Edward can scarcely have overlooked this fact. But he assumed that Bruce, with his growing power, would take the castles before long and defend them against him. This was a fairly reasonable conclusion, for it was the normal course of warfare in those days. Battles were fought for the possession of castles. When one side had won them all, and the other side had failed to retake them, the war was over. Edward, whose father had given him a good military education, never doubted that this war would follow the customary pattern. Louden Hill and Loch Etive should have taught him that Robert Bruce did not follow patterns but originated them.

Bruce was not without his intelligence sources in England. Word of the invincible siege-train reached him even as Edward was summoning his master gibbet-builders. He moved, at first, very much as the English King expected him to. In November, 1312, he set out to conquer the formidable stronghold of Perth.

Perth was a fair-sized town, walled in stone and protected by a deep moat running all around the outside. The castle, set inside the town, was a massive fortress, doubly strong because of this outer ring of defense. Its governor was Sir William Oliphant, a Baliol man who preferred English rule to the hated Bruce. He scornfully refused a demand to surrender, and Bruce sat down to try to starve him out.

For six weeks in the winter cold he camped outside the town, intercepting food supplies when he could. However, the garrison was well-provisioned, and if anyone went hungry it was only the innocent townspeople. Bruce's own men suffered far more from hunger and cold than the besieged in their snug castle.

Christmas Day came, with little holiday spirit in the shivering Bruce camp. James Douglas, ever a lover of good food, sighed as he finished his dish of porridge, washed down with cold water. Lord James was suffering from a broken arm and inclined to be a little peevish.

"This can't go on forever, Robert," he said. "We've been here for six weeks now, and the English laugh at us. I hate to say it, but Perth is too tough a nut to crack. Let's go back to Methven, where at least we can find a bit of mutton."

Bruce, who had eaten the poor fare without comment, shook his head. "It's a tough nut, but we have to crack it, James. We can't leave these English garrisons scattered about the country to give aid and comfort to Edward when he comes. There *must* be a way into Perth! Can't you think of one, James? Or you, Thomas?"

The young Earl of Moray flushed with pleasure at being consulted. Thomas Randolph, although he had earned it by valor in the field, was not yet quite accustomed to the warm friendliness of his late captors. He did not doubt that his uncle had forgiven his defiant attitude, but he was always eager to earn forgiveness anew.

He knit his brows now and came up with a diffident question. "How deep is the moat around the city wall?"

Douglas laughed. "Bottomless, the farmers say. Why?"

"Well, I was thinking." Randolph looked across at the wall, grim solid stone in the deepening twilight. Beyond it, toward the center of the town, loomed the high tower of Perth Castle.

"If we could get into the town," the boy went on, "we might not have to worry about taking the castle. The governor would have to come down and fight us in the streets, wouldn't he? That's what I'd do in his place, anyway."

Robert smiled at him. "And you'd be quite right, Tommy. Oliphant is too good a soldier to try to hold a castle set in a captured town. Once we're inside the walls—! The only question is, how do we get inside?"

"The walls are not so high," Douglas put in. "With even the smallest of Edward's siege-gibbets, we could step across them. But of course we poverty-stricken Scots have no gibbets!"

The King motioned him to silence. "Well, Tommy?"

The boy scowled in furious concentration. "If we had some ladders—if we could row across the moat—no, it's too narrow for that. And we haven't any boats, either. We could swim it, but how could we do that and carry ladders? Oh, I give up, Uncle. James is right, this is too tough a nut to crack."

"I'm not so sure." Bruce's eyes kindled. "You've set me thinking, Tommy, or your first question has. Do you remember a moment ago you asked 'How deep is the moat?'"

"And James said it was bottomless, Uncle."

"Ah, but does James know that? Does anybody know it for sure?" Bruce got lightly to his feet. "Bring your spear, Nephew. You and I are going to find out."

Full darkness had fallen now. Wrapping their plaids against the cutting Christmas wind, uncle and nephew set out to follow the moat's circle around the town.

They slipped and slid on the snowy bank as they prodded with their spears at the stagnant black water. For most of the way they could not touch bottom. They had almost concluded the circle back to camp when they came upon a short stretch where fallen masonry had filled the ditch so that the water was no more than five feet deep. They marked the spot and hurried home.

The next morning, in full view of the sentries on the wall, the Scots packed up and retreated to Methven, their base some miles away. Oliphant sat down to write to his King that Bruce had acknowledged failure, retreating without even attempting an assault.

Methven, the little town that had seen his first defeat, was Bruce's headquarters for this region. He had no master carpenters like Edward's, but he set his men to fashioning rough ladders, a task not beyond their skill. Young trees were cut down and stripped, their branches lashed across them for steps. The ladders were flimsy, but they were light to carry and strong enough to hold a man.

In the second week of the new year, 1313, Bruce and his men again approached Perth. They hid in the woods until dark. Then, one by one, each fully armed man carrying a ladder over his head, they stole down to the moat.

Bruce, with Randolph close behind him, was first to plunge into the icy black water, foul with the town's garbage. It swirled around him up to the neck, but he waded safely across and set up his ladder against the wall. Oliphant, thinking the danger of siege past, had reduced the number of watchmen, so that no alarm was given. Silently the Scots swarmed over, to waken the sleeping town with their wild war cry.

Oliphant, as Randolph had predicted, ordered his men into the streets, where a fierce sharp battle raged.

The commander himself was wounded, and surrendered. Bruce entered the castle without difficulty, to replace the English flag with the Scottish royal standard.

So far he had acted much as Edward would have expected him to act. But, when morning came, he took his own genius-inspired way. The frightened townspeople were assured that they had nothing to fear. They were Scots, even though they had served the English, and their own Scottish King would deal gently with them. He would show his good will by providing them with employment at generous wages. Every able-bodied man was ordered to report to the castle, bringing spades, pickaxes, and wheelbarrows.

Under Bruce's directions, the men of Perth spent the next few weeks destroying their town's military installations. The wall was thrown down, its stones used to fill up the moat. The castle walls, trundled stone by stone in wheelbarrows, went to swell the ring of piled rocks where once water had flowed. The villagers worked well and were generously paid, according to the King's promise. It might be said that Edward of England paid them, for the money came out of Oliphant's strongbox.

So, while Edward's mobilization creaked on, Bruce was surging across Scotland, capturing and destroying the strong points on which Scottish wars had focused for centuries. Perth was the first of a triumphant series.

Around the Taking of the Castles a dozen good stories cluster, all of them stirring and romantic, and some of them not very plausible.

Douglas, who rather specialized in castle-taking, is the hero of many of them. Once he is supposed to have draped his men in cowskins and led them, crawling on all fours, up to a castle gate. The meat-hungry inmates opened their doors to the heaven-sent herd of cattle, and got themselves slaughtered for their greediness.

Thomas Randolph also had his triumphs. He captured Edinburgh Castle with the help of a soldier who had once loved a maiden living there and knew a secret route to her window. Then there was William Bunnock, of whom nothing else is known, but who took Linlithgow by a ruse that has passed into Scottish folklore. Bunnock drove a haycart to the castle gate, saying the governor had ordered it. When the portcullis lifted to admit him, he stopped his cart directly under it, stabbed the porter, and let the portcullis fall, jammed by the load of hay. His comrades poured through the opening, and Linlithgow Peel fell to their spears.

In one way or another, usually by strategy and almost never by direct assault, Bruce ran up his flag over the castles and then destroyed them. By the end of 1313, exactly five of them remained, intact and still in enemy hands. These were all concentrated in a small area near the border, on the eastern coast. Except for this hostile region, all Scotland was his, and united behind him. He was ready, or as nearly ready as he could ever hope to be, for the decisive trial of strength that must come when Edward finally began his invasion.

❦ ❦ XVII ❦ ❦

EDWARD II OF ENGLAND moved north in late spring, reaching Berwick on June 1, 1314. A week later he crossed the border and led his army up the old Roman road that thrust straight and broad into the heart of Scotland.

It must have been a magnificent sight. His famous train was made up of 106 four-horse wagons and 110 eight-ox ones. The wagons carried siege-engines, spare weapons and armor, and a huge amount of foodstuffs. There was load after load of Edward's personal possessions: silk-and-velvet tents, beds and armchairs, gold plate and fine wines, delicate foods and French perfume and down cushions. Escorting the wagons was the heavy cavalry, a service arm which his father had brought to the peak of perfection.

A heavy cavalryman was actually heavy in himself, being chosen for weight, as was his horse. The horses were a special breed, massive and slow-moving, the ancestors of the truck horses still occasionally seen on our city streets. The cavalry horses had their own armor, great blankets of chain mail. A burly cavalryman, armored and mounted on his armored horse, weighed something over a ton.

The light cavalry troops rode smaller, swifter horses, more suitable for maneuver. These animals were protected only by quilted cotton blankets, although their riders wore chain mail. Common horse-soldiers were heavy or light cavalrymen, and remained either one or the other. But the King and his knights had both heavy horses and light ones, changing from one to another as circumstances dictated.

Figures of different historians vary widely, but the lowest estimate of Edward's strength gives him twenty-five hundred heavy cavalry, five thousand light, and fifteen thousand infantrymen. He must have had two or three thousand officers, for every landowner who furnished his complement of fighting-men was expected to command them in person. There were innumerable grooms, wagon-drivers, and servants, and we know that Edward brought twenty minstrels with harp and lute, for the express purpose of composing songs to celebrate the expected victories.

His officer corps included nearly every noble, English

and Scottish, who had a special grudge against Bruce.
Lord Pembroke was there, the man Bruce defeated at
Loudon Hill. So, also, was Sir Robert de Clifford, for
whose edification Douglas had prepared the Larder.
There were several Comyns, among them Sir John, son
of the Red John whom Bruce had slain at Dumfries.

The list glittered, too, with the great names of England, among them those of the barons who had murdered Gaveston. Not all of these nobles were present in
person. Lancaster and a few others stayed at home to
keep their grip on the government, delegating sons or
nephews to represent them.

This was the mighty war machine, the steam roller
that Edward had painstakingly builded for the final
crushing of the Scottish rebellion. Eight years had gone
by since Isabella Buchan had placed the homemade
crown on Bruce's head, seven since Edward had promised his dying father to "head or hang" the Beggar King.
With all the strength that he could muster, Edward had
come at last to keep his promise.

To oppose him, Bruce had fewer than eight thousand
men, about five hundred of them mounted on tough little farm ponies. Pitifully small though it seemed against
Edward's numbers, this was yet the largest force Bruce
had ever commanded. It was composed, not of sullen
vassals blindly following their lords, but of sturdy Scots

who knew what they were fighting for, every man of them.

The clan system in Scotland was very different from the feudalism of England. Even in the peaceful past, the Scottish court had never been the sort of gay social center that England and the European capitals knew. The lords lived on their lands, closer to their tenants and often bound to them by ties of blood. In a country with so little national wealth, the distinction between gentlemen and commoner was less sharply drawn. A Scottish noble did not think it beneath him to lend a hand in his hayfields or to give his daughter in marriage to a stout yeoman. There was consequently a warmer feeling, a deeper comradeship, among the men who followed Bruce, and a more intelligent understanding of the issues.

In the matter of morale, Bruce had a distinct advantage over his English enemy, whose army was made up of bickering factions. He had also a superior knowledge of the land, and the loyal support of the leaders under him. These were all intangibles, and a lesser man would have found them cold comfort when the English legions came into view. But Bruce, if he felt a moment's discouragement, never gave any evidence of it.

He learned that Edward was making for Stirling Castle, one of the last strongholds still in English hands.

Edward Bruce had already tried and failed to take it. Its governor was the Sir Geoffrey de Moubray who had fared so badly at Glentrool. Bruce resolved that at all costs the English army must be stopped outside the gates of Stirling.

He chose the battleground deliberately, disposing his little force so that the land itself would fight for him. It was about three miles south of Stirling Castle, where the ancient Roman road crossed a small stream known as Bannockburn, at a village of the same name.

Between the castle and the brook was the New Park, a thickly wooded tract reserved by some forgotten Scots king for deer-hunting. Outside the belt of trees there was grassy meadowland, broken on the northern bank of the brook by two marshes, soggy with peat.

The brook itself, although on level land where the road crossed it, ran eastward into a deep narrow gorge nearly a mile long. Where the gorge ended, there was a second crossing, with a bridle path leading up to the castle. The brook was not deep, so that at both spots it was possible to ford it.

Bruce reached the northern bank of the Bannockburn two days ahead of Edward, who was coming up from the south. He camped in the New Park woods and began his preparations for battle.

The meadowland just outside the belt of trees would

make an excellent battleground, from the enemy's point of view. There was firm footing there, and room for the dreaded heavy cavalry to stage one of their irresistible charges. Bruce quickly determined that the field must be made unusable for them.

He set his men to digging pits in the ground, "as round as a man's head and as deep as his knee." When the meadow was honeycombed with holes, he had sticks laid across them and covered with the original grassy sod. To the eye, there was no difference. The meadow seemed as smooth as before, but now it was a series of traps for enemy horses. Where it ended, the bog began. This "mined" meadow figures largely in many romantic accounts of the battle. The sad truth is that it was never used. The actual fighting occurred more than a mile to the east of the Roman road, at the second ford.

On Sunday morning, June 23, Mass was celebrated beneath the trees that sheltered the Scottish camp. When the service ended, trumpets blared, and the troops fell in for their final inspection and battle orders. Bruce, mounted on a little gray pony, rode up and down the lines, making sure that every man understood the part he was to play, and was ready for it.

If the Bruce forces lacked the glitter of the gilt and silver armor so conspicuous among the advancing foe, they had still a wealth of homely Scottish color. Twenty-one clan chieftains had rallied to the Bruce. They stood, each at the head of his men, dressed in the distinctive plaid of the family. There were Campbells and Douglases, Stewarts and Drummonds, Rosses and Keiths, Fergusons and Robertsons, and many another famous name.

The vivid blues and yellows, the reds and greens, of the chiefs' cloaks were repeated in the mantles or kilts of their followers. Bruce himself, in full armor, wore a linen tunic embroidered with his coat of arms over his steel-link shirt, with a mantle of the Bruce tartan, red and blue cross-barred by thin lines of yellow and white. Most of the chiefs had adequate armor, but many of the common soldiers had to rely on cowhide jackets, tough enough to blunt an arrow-point. Except for whatever bit of plaid a man could manage, there was no attempt at uniforms.

The King's inspection was brief but thorough. When it ended, he wheeled his little horse to face them all, and a hushed silence fell. It was broken by a calm, earnest voice speaking immortal words.

"Men of Scotland! This is the hour of choosing. If there be one among you whose heart fails him, let him now depart. For, on my honor, I will have no man at my side this day who holds his life dearer than freedom. Is there such a man here? Speak!"

The answer came back in a thunderous "No!" It was minutes before the shouting died and Bruce could continue. His voice was steady, and very solemn.

"You know, as I know, that many among us will not see the setting of tomorrow's sun. It may be that we shall all die, for our enemy is mighty. I do not attempt to tell you that the chances are equal. We have not a fifth part of the numbers or the weapons that the English tyrant has mustered against us. He will ride us down with horse, he will hurl stones and arrows against us. To oppose him we have only the strength of our bodies, and of our hearts.

"Yet I would remind you of another time when Scots stood in like case at a spot not far from here. You all remember the battle of Stirling Bridge. Wallace, too, faced overwhelming odds, and by God's grace won through to victory. So may it be with us, if our hearts are strong. And, for their strengthening, repeat with me now the motto our martyred Wallace gave his men. You know it well. 'God—' "

"God armeth the patriot!"

The mighty shout shook the hot June air. A very few of the men in the ranks had served with Wallace. Not many, for most of the dead leader's followers had shared his fate. But to every man there the name was a sacred one, and this reminder of how Wallace had scattered Surrey's superior force at Stirling Bridge brought new courage. With heads held high, stepping proudly to the lively strains of the bagpipes, the clansmen moved off to take up their assigned positions.

The summer air, even under the trees, was very warm. Bruce felt the weight of his steel helmet, and had just replaced it with a light leather cap when Douglas rode in from a scouting expedition. Earlier in the morning he had been sent across Bannock Brook to see how close the enemy might be. He was hot and dusty as he slid down from his horse before the King's tent.

"Oh, you're back, James." Bruce handed the helmet to his page and came out from the rough shelter of sailcloth they had stretched for him.

"Sit here in the shade. The boy will take your horse. Well, let's have the news. How near are they?"

"Too near," Douglas answered soberly. "Look, you can see for yourself. That cloud of dust on the horizon there—it stretches back as far as the eye can reach. Never in my life, Robert, have I seen so many men, or such a wealth of armament. It's like a tide of the ocean, sweeping irresistibly down upon us. We won't find it easy to turn back that tide, my King."

"We never thought it would be easy," Bruce answered briskly. "Come now, James, I didn't send you out to report the size of Edward's army. That we knew already. The point is, when will they reach the ford? How long have we to prepare for battle?"

"I can only guess. They are moving slowly, because of the heat and their great weight. Unless they quicken their pace, the main body will not reach the ford before nightfall. But there is a troop of light cavalry leading the way—I saw the banner of my old enemy de Clifford floating over it. They could reach us, if they put spurs to their horses, in a couple of hours. I don't suppose they would engage us, though, until the heavy cavalry comes up."

"I shouldn't think so. Still, it's hard to guess the enemy's plans. You have a score to settle with Clifford, James?"

Douglas laughed. "I think we might say he has a score to settle with me. I left him the Douglas Larder, didn't I? No, I've no private grudges to satisfy, Robert. Sir Robert de Clifford is a brave man and a good soldier. He fights for his King, as I fight for mine. May the best cause win!"

"Spoken like a true knight, James." Bruce smiled, but his anxious eyes did not leave the horizon, where the dust-cloud was almost blotting out blue sky. For a few minutes the two sat in silence. Then, rather wearily, the King rose to his feet.

"I think you'd better join your men, Douglas. As you know, they're posted back along the road, between here and the castle. They went off under that young kinsman of yours, James Stewart's boy. I don't know what sort of a commander he'd make them if the need came."

"Young Walter? He'll make a fine commander, Robert. It's true the boy hasn't seen battle yet. But he's hardy and strong, a skilled mountain climber and a fool for danger. When he came in last week with his twenty Highlanders, I could have jumped for joy. You'll be glad of young Walter Stewart before we're done, if I know anything about men."

"And who knows more? If you think well of him, that's enough for me. Get along with you now, James. I'll see you again this afternoon, when I make my rounds."

❧ ❧ XVIII ❧ ❧

BY EARLY AFTERNOON the English were in plain sight, pouring into the meadow on the south side of the brook. Apparently they meant to make camp there, for the columns had halted and dispersed. Servants were scurrying about, setting up tents and gathering peat for firemaking. The little stream was muddied by the hoofs of battle chargers led down to drink, and the clang of discarded weapons mingled with good-natured shouts as weary men settled themselves to rest.

Bruce, no more than half a mile away, watched from a knoll known as the Borestone. As the tents went up, he could make out the standards of half a dozen English nobles, men who had shared his boyhood days at King Edward's court. He had met these men in combat before, the mock combat of the tourney, where one knight strives against another for a lady's smile. Now, by the hard necessity of war, he was to meet these old friends in grim earnest, with his life or theirs the forfeit.

He sighed a little, and turned away. Such thoughts were not pleasant. Better to get on with the business in hand. He mounted his horse and galloped off for a final inspection.

The most forward outpost, commanded by Edward Bruce, lay very close to the brook's edge. It was well screened by trees and low-growing bushes, but as Bruce approached it he was momentarily exposed to view from the opposite bank. His great height and flaming red hair attracted the attention of a young English knight, one Sir Henry de Bohun, just riding into camp.

Sir Henry recognized Bruce and acted immediately. Setting spurs to his horse, he galloped across the burn and confronted the man his King had sworn to kill. What dreams of glory burned in his rash young brain we can well imagine. If he could kill or capture the Bruce, alone, singlehanded, almost in Edward's presence, there would be no reward too rich for asking. It was a bold venture, and came shudderingly close to success.

De Bohun, fully armed and armored, riding a heavy armored battle steed, bore down upon Robert on his little gray pony. The King, who had left his helmet in his tent, had left his sword there, too, when he started on this brief tour of inspection. The only weapon he had with him was the battle-ax that swung from his saddlebow. From his brother Edward, crouching in the bushes at the side of the road, came a curse that was more like a prayer. The men with him held their breath, and even the English camp fell silent to watch.

De Bohun's horse splashed through the brook and clattered up the stony road that had echoed to the tramp of Roman legions. Bruce, pulled up beside the path, raised the ax high above his head. As the Englishman's horse plunged past, he rose in his stirrups and brought the ax down full upon de Bohun's head. The keen blade, with all that power behind it, clove straight through steel and bone, and de Bohun's brief dream of glory flickered out in bloody death.

So, in single combat, opened the memorable battle of Bannockburn. Its full fury was not to break until the following day. But, before the Sunday dusk fell, the Scots had still another triumph to add to the one their King had given them.

Douglas's old enemy de Clifford, some time in the afternoon, stole away from the English camp with his light-horse troop and crossed the brook by the lower ford. Screened by hill and wood, he followed the bridle path that led up to Stirling Castle. He was halfway there when Randolph discovered him and attacked.

The Scots were afoot, formed into the famous "schiltrom," rings within rings of kneeling spearmen, with their archers in the center. The spears, thrust upward from near the ground, pierced the horses, and the arrows found the riders. Time after time the English rode straight at the wall of bristling spears, only to reel back again. The summer sun beat down on bleeding, sweating men, on maddened horses trampling their fallen riders into the ground, and on the final flight of Clifford and the handful left to him.

Edward of England had sent no men to relieve the unfortunate de Clifford. The English army, on the south side of the burn, proceeded to settle down for the night. Their numbers were so great that the camp, to avail itself of water, had to be strung out more than a mile along the brook. This brought the farthest section past the gorge to the east, and past where the gorge ended. It was at this far end of the gorge that the bridle path crossed the burn and ran to Stirling Castle. Clifford, although he had no luck there, had fought Randolph on a firm stretch of meadowland to the east of the New Park woods.

This was not the meadow that Bruce had mined with pits. That tract lay to the west of the Roman road and never figured in the two-days' fighting. All the action, both the Randolph-Clifford engagement on Sunday and the great battle of the following day, took place east of the road, in the wood and the meadow beyond it. Like

many another general, Bruce found his carefully prepared battle plan upset and was forced to improvise a
new one in the field. His genius showed in the fact that
the spur-of-the-moment plan was even better than the
old one.

On both sides of the Bannock, that fateful Midsummer's Eve, the campfires lighted up a grave council of
war. Edward's generals reported that the men were
restive and uneasy. They had seen de Clifford's crack
cavalry regiment broken and dispersed by men on
foot, a thing that simply did not happen in their experience.

If a similar miracle had favored their side, they
would have attributed it to the intervention of the saints.
Since it was the enemy who benefited, they were convinced that the devil had a hand in it. The Prince of
Darkness was a very real person in medieval thinking,
with vast powers and a lively interest in human affairs.
It seemed quite plausible to the English soldiers that the
Scots had enlisted him on their side. This belief was a
contributing factor to the demoralization of the English
troops next day.

Edward did his best, sending heralds through the
camp to make a brave show of reassurance. The heralds'
ringing words were supplemented by a generous issue

of ale, and the murmuring quieted. The officers were invited to the royal tent for a feast, there to drown whatever fears they might entertain.

On the Scottish side there was no feasting. It was the eve of St. John's Day, when good Christians traditionally abstained from meat and wine. Since the Bruce army had neither, they cannot have found it too difficult to keep the fast. The more devout among them passed the night in prayer, led by the venerable Abbot of Inchaffray. At dawn the entire host knelt for Mass and received the Abbot's blessing on their undertaking.

Long before the dawn, Bruce had gathered his closest leaders about him in his tent on the Borestone. Edward's servants had set up a handsome striped pavilion, hung with tapestry, on the bank of Bannockburn. The King of Scots invited his friends to sit beneath a patched length of sailcloth strung between two trees. It was literally the only home he owned.

They took their places on the dew-wet grass. James Douglas, a great dark giant of a man with laughing eyes. His cousin Walter Stewart, shy and silent, with hero-worshiping eyes fixed on Bruce's face. Thomas Randolph, flushed with victory, and a little inclined to swagger about it. Edward Bruce, grim, unsmiling, not too well pleased at Randolph's obvious satisfaction. And in the midst of them, sitting cross-legged on the grass, his huge freckled knees protruding from the red and blue kilt of Bruce tartan, the red-haired King.

"Sirs," he began when all were present, "our good friend Randolph has given us a heartening victory. I have called you here to discuss our plan for tomorrow. What shall it be?"

Randolph spoke quickly. "Naturally, the same as today. Let them come on! We'll take them as they come. And before tomorrow's sun sets, I'll have Edward fleeing as Clifford fled today."

Douglas cast a puzzled look at his King. "Is there any question, Robert? We're in a good position here, far better than we'd be if we let the English get past to the castle. What can we do but stand and fight it out?"

"Another suggestion has been offered," the King replied. "Edward, tell the others what you said to me a few minutes ago."

Edward Bruce's heavy face did not lighten. "I said Randolph's victory was enough to go on with. It has given the English a useful lesson. Let's not tempt fate too far. We can retire, laying the countryside waste before their advance, harassing them from ambush. That's the kind of fighting we're best at, and the English worst. Why should we meet them in pitched battle, where they excel? We're only inviting annihilation. I say let's be off while there is still time."

An excited protest rose from Randolph and Douglas, but Bruce said mildly, "Edward's point is one we must consider. All our fighting strength is assembled here. All our leaders are here. If we give battle now, and the tide goes against us, we are ruined. Shall we take this desperate chance?"

"Why not?" Randolph cut in. "Mine was a desperate chance today, and it succeeded."

Young Walter Stewart cleared his throat. "Yours was a desperate chance against de Bohun, my lord King. Yet you did not flinch from it."

Edward Bruce made an impatient gesture. "Those were chances that had to be taken, both of them. Neither you, Robert, nor Randolph had a choice. But here we do have a choice. We could steal away before the dawn, drawing Edward deeper into the country, fighting as we have fought before, and with no small success. Oh, don't misunderstand me, it's not retreat I'm counseling! I speak from prudence, not from fear. And if any man here thinks otherwise—" he glared at Randolph, "—I'll be glad to meet him in combat."

"That will do, Brother." Bruce's tone was suddenly stern. "No one has questioned your courage. We have no time for foolish quarrels among ourselves. Now, as to this advice you have given. I think myself it is good, although I am very reluctant to take it. However, the matter is not for one man to decide, nor five men. Walter, call all the chiefs of all the clans. We'll put it to them."

Quickly the chieftains assembled, crowding about the King. In calm, level tones he laid Edward's suggestion before them, giving no hint of his own opinion. The men, who had heartily cheered Bruce's "death or glory" speech of the night before, listened with puzzled faces. There was silence for a minute when he finished, and then a gnarled old Highlander asked bluntly, "Is this your wish, sir King?"

"I'd rather know your wishes, Duncan."

"Well—" the old man hesitated, and looked at the serious faces around him. "It doesn't seem to me it's for us to say. We swore to follow where you lead. You're our King; where you go we'll go. But I'm of no mind to turn tail now. That I will say."

"And I'll say it too!" someone in the crowd shouted, and a chorus of deep voices took up the assent. Douglas and Randolph joined it, and young Stewart. Only Edward Bruce remained grimly silent.

King Robert drew a long breath. "You've spoken as I hoped to hear you to speak. Perhaps it would be wiser to wait and let this weary war drag on, as it has done for so many years. But I think the time has come to put our fortunes to the test. We have been victorious today. God helping us, we shall go on as we have begun!"

With the final decision taken, he proceeded to outline the new plan of battle. From the disposition of the English camp, it seemed unlikely that the attempt to cross would be made by the Roman road, as had first been expected.

Far down the brook, where the gorge ended, there was an easy crossing, as de Clifford had found out, and an open meadow all the way up to Stirling Castle. Bruce did not leave the road unguarded, but he posted his main strength in the wood that edged the grassland.

King Edward was astir at dawn, watching his army gather itself for the advance. Then, glancing across the brook, he saw a strange sight. A detachment of Scots, with banners flying and bagpipes skirling, was pouring out of the wood and into the meadow. They were all on foot, and they were led by Edward Bruce, who had demanded this perilous honor to show that his caution the night before had not been dictated by cowardice.

From the English point of view, this exposure in the open was too good to be true. They had expected to have to engage the Scots in the woods, where neither cavalry nor archery operated to the best advantage. The sight of Edward Bruce's command recklessly venturing upon the plain was too tempting to ignore. The trumpets sounded, and English cavalry thundered across the brook.

Using the schiltrom formation that had defeated Clifford, the Scots stood solidly against the onslaught, a bristling hedgehog of spears. Clifford had fought on higher ground nearer the castle, and his horses had been light and quick on their feet. The meadow here, where it ran down to the brook, was marshy, and soon cut up by floundering hoofs. Long before he had buckled on his armor and mounted his own horse, the English King realized that his heavy cavalry was in serious trouble.

He galloped up and down the camp, shouting for reinforcements to follow. The very size of his army made for confusion. There was in addition a great deal of jealousy among the noble officers, two of whom stopped long enough for a private duel to decide which should have the place of honor at the King's side.

The lay of the land added to the difficulties. The deep gorge made it impossible to cross the brook on a wide front, so that the ford was choked with a shoving, bumping mass of men and horses. The common soldiers, responsible only to their own lords, found themselves separated from their units and refused to take orders from strange officers. The press was so great that two hundred knights never drew their swords. This was not from cowardice, but simply because they were never able to get within arm's reach of an enemy.

The Bruce forces, disciplined and ready, suffered from no such confusion. Even as Edward Bruce's spearmen drew first blood, new divisions swarmed out from the wood. The agile little ponies of Sir Robert Keith's mounted troop danced about the heavy English chargers, giving their riders a dozen points of vantage from which to strike. And behind the scanty cavalry arm came wave on wave of foot soldiers shouting their Gaelic battle cries, brandishing ax and spear and the dreaded claymore.

The English were pushed upstream along the northern bank, closer and closer to the cliff. Hundreds of them were crowded over and died on the sharp rocks of the brook's bed below. One of Edward's minstrels, in a song condoning the defeat, explained that Bruce's friend Satan appeared in person at a crucial moment in the battle and opened this fatal cleft in the earth. The minstrel was very positive about it, claiming that he had heard the rock split and smelled brimstone with his own nose. The entire English army had camped beside the gorge all night and must have known it was there, but no one contradicted the story. It still turns up in some English histories, although Bruce rather than the devil is credited with digging the ditch while the English slept. It was fifty feet deep, cut in sheer rock, and would have provided a busy night's work even for the energetic Scots.

Edward of England, a fool but no coward, plunged into the scrimmage and acquitted himself bravely. But by early afternoon his generals were urging him to save himself. That he should be taken prisoner was unthinkable, but as things were going it was a looming possibility.

Hugh le Despenser, a young knight who was soon to take the place of the lamented Gaveston, succeeded in persuading him. With a few hundred horsemen, Edward took Clifford's bridle path to Stirling. The escort was commanded by Sir Giles de Argentine, a courageous knight who had once been Bruce's friend. At the castle gate Sir Giles curtly told his King, "I am not used to flee, and I will not now." He rode back to the battle, and perished there.

Stirling, which must soon yield to Bruce, offered no shelter for the English King. After a brief rest he pressed on to the coast and there found a ship to take him back to England.

Seeing their King in flight, the English lost what little heart they had. Their demoralization was completed by a new horde of men who burst yelling out of the woods. These were the "gillies," or servants, a motley crowd of hostlers and cooks who had been left in the camp. They had blackened their faces with soot, snatched up shovels and pitchforks, and come of their own will to join the fight. To the superstitious English soldiers, already far gone in panic, they were visible devils from hell, let loose by their infernal master. The panic became a rout, and hundreds were crushed and trampled in the wild flight that ended a day of horror and of glory.

The day was June 24, 1314. It is a day whose memory lives on in Scottish hearts, and will not die while freedom lives.

❦ ❦ XIX ❦ ❦

CASTLE and camp both fell to the victors. Bruce gave his men a free hand for looting, and the simple Scots had a wonderful time dressing up in velvet and eating Edward's imported pickled lampreys from Edward's silver-gilt plates. More important was the huge store of army food and spare weapons. The Scottish army naturally fell heir to all the beautiful siege-engines and gibbets, never used and as good as new.

Valuable though all this treasure was, the battle provided an even richer source of ready cash. When the prisoners were sorted out and counted, it was found that five hundred of them were of high rank. This meant five hundred ransoms.

Among the captives was one man who purchased his freedom without spending a cent, simply by exercising his literary talent. He was one of Edward's twenty minstrels: not the one who had smelled brimstone, but a very accomplished poet named Baston.

The king's minstrels accompanied him to war as combined reporters and press agents. It was their duty to observe what went on and to put it into verse. The job was well paid, and carried a great deal of prestige. Naturally enough, a minstrel who wanted to remain on the payroll did not present his patron in an unfavorable light, no matter what happened. If by any chance the royal arms suffered reverses, a smooth-tongued poet could always find excuses and explanations. A victory, of course, was invariably won by the king's own daring and wisdom, and no praise was too extravagant.

Baston, with nineteen competitors to worry about, had determined to be first with his Bannockburn epic. He sat up all night before the battle, getting the manuscript into shape. He left a few blanks for details, but he described the battlefield and the attack accurately enough, with a glowing description of the mighty English cavalry charge. Actually, the poet's imagination anticipated the battle very much as it occurred, except for the important detail of which side won.

Baston's captor was young Walter Stewart, something of a poet himself. He read the manuscript with sincere admiration and made the author a sporting proposition. If he would rewrite it from the actual facts, and make as good a job of it, he might go free.

The poet eagerly agreed, and within the space of three

hours produced a revised version that turned the Scottish minstrels green with envy. The gratified Baston, having found in Stewart an appreciation that Edward lacked, refused to return to England and established himself as the Stewart family minstrel.

The most important prisoner, in the matter of rank, was the Earl of Hereford, de Bohun's uncle. This gentleman was one of the murderers of Piers Gaveston. It is not likely that Edward II would have lifted a hand to save him, but Lady Hereford appealed to Parliament. The barons who made up that body, several of them co-murderers in the Gaveston killing, were sympathetic to her plea. As a surer argument than mere money, they gave her fifteen prisoners to bargain with.

In exchange for her husband's safe return, the Countess of Hereford offered Bruce his wife and daughter, his two sisters, a nephew, and Bishop Wishart. For good measure, the Countess threw in a few Scottish ladies who had been captured later. There was no mention of Isabella Buchan, presumably dead now and long forgotten.

The negotiations were successfully concluded. Late in October Bruce rode down to the border with a company of cavalry. The captive Earl of Hereford, his sword restored to him, rode at the King's side, together with Neil Campbell and Walter Stewart. Douglas did not come, for he was enthusiastically trying out the captured siege weapons against Bothwell Castle, which did not long resist them. Randolph was busy supervising the destruction of Stirling Castle. Edward Bruce came along to welcome his sisters.

The autumn sun beat down on a glittering spectacle. For once, the haughty English would have no chance to sneer at the homespun Scots. The loot of Bannockburn was everywhere in evidence. Mounted on English horses, their rusty armor replaced by shining English steel, cloaks of English velvet swinging from their shoulders, the Scottish knights deliberately flaunted the fruits of victory. Edward had told his story by this time, with all the excuses his minstrels could concoct, but here was the incontrovertible evidence of his defeat.

They came to a halt just outside Berwick town, and Bruce's heralds sounded a summons. They were answered by English trumpeters on the walls, and slowly the city gates swung open. A company of cavalry clattered out and drew up about a hundred yards from the Scottish troop. In their midst could be seen several women on horseback, and a litter swung between two horses.

There was a long wait, for neither side quite trusted the other. Then Bruce turned impatiently to Hereford.

"Go, my lord, and God go with you. You are free."
The prisoner raised his hand in courtly salute, and cantered forward. As he moved, there was movement in the opposite company. An old white horse, spurred by an eager rider, broke from the group and plunged straight for the spot where Bruce's red hair gleamed. It was the Princess Marjorie.

Bruce slid from his mount just in time to take her into his arms. When last he had seen his daughter she had been an awkward child of ten, freckled and rawboned like himself. She was a grown-up young lady now, and very lovely. But the sunny smile was the same, and the impetuous affection with which she launched herself at her father was unchanged.

In a moment the other exiles surrounded him. His widowed sister Christina, gaunt and pale but proudly presenting her tall son, who like Marjorie had grown up in eight long years of confinement. Mary Bruce, the harmless little mouse who had suffered most unjustly of all, but who at least had a living husband to comfort her. Neil Campbell, with an indignant glance at the sorry horse the English had given her, swept her up to his own saddlebow and held her close.

Lady Hereford had been rather niggardly in her provision of horses for the prisoners. The first word Bruce heard from his wife was a word of complaint.

Elizabeth, Queen of Scots, pushed her stepdaughter aside to give her husband a perfunctory kiss.

"I think you ought to do something about it, Robert," she began. "You know yourself I was riding a good horse when I left you. Nothing like this bag of bones! They took my poor Sandy away, but they ought to give me another one as good. Don't you think so, Robert?"

And then, abandoning one grievance among so many, she burst into angry tears.

"It isn't just the horse, it's everything! Do you know what they allowed me for my keep, Robert? Twenty shillings a week. Think of it! Twenty miserable shillings. Look at me, I'm in rags. I haven't had a new gown in all these eight years, and my shoes are in patches. Oh, Robert, I'm so unhappy!"

Weeping she had left him, and weeping she returned. He let her pour out all her tale of petty wrongs, patting her heaving shoulders with awkward tenderness. Not so would Isabella Buchan, the valiant-hearted, have come back to him. Perhaps this thought crossed his mind, and perhaps it did not. We have no way of knowing.

It must have been with relief that he turned to the litter from which Bishop Wishart's quavering voice called to him. The saintly old man, who had kindled the first spark of resistance in Wallace, who had guided and counseled Bruce in the difficult early days, who had shriven him when he came red-handed from Dumfries Cloister—Bishop Wishart shed no tears. He was nearly ninety now, broken from prison rigors, his eyesight gone and his death-day not far off. But he greeted Bruce with calm cheerfulness, making only one request.

"Tell me when we cross the border, Son. I shall not see Scotch earth again, but I must know when it is under my feet. Then I can die in peace."

With another flourish of trumpets, the English troop re-entered the city gate, which closed behind them. Bruce, before he could leave, was obliged to shift the Queen's sidesaddle to a soldier's good horse. The better to dry her tears, he wrapped her in the gold-bordered purple mantle that had once belonged to King Edward.

The cavalcade rode back to Stirling, where Bruce was making his headquarters. Traveling by easy stages, for the old Bishop's sake, they took two days for the journey. It was noted among the knights that Walter Stewart, although splendidly mounted, subdued his spirited horse to the slow-paced hack that had been given to Princess Marjorie. A prisoner since her tenth year, the girl had had no opportunity to practice horsemanship, and young Sir Walter made a delightful teacher.

Stirling Castle was a ruin, and Bruce had no suitable home to offer his aggrieved lady. He fitted up a smaller castle near by, Clackmannan, with all the English linen and cushions he could lay hands on, and wrested Edward's gold plate from the reluctant Randolph, who believed that finders are keepers. Even with these luxuries, Clackmannan was a gloomy, comfortless place. Elizabeth complained a good deal about the hard life she had come home to, when all her sufferings clearly entitled her to a soft one.

Bruce had not much time to listen to his wife's woes. Like everyone else, he had supposed that his overwhelming victory over the massed English army meant an end to the war. By any sort of sound reasoning it should have done so. Not again in Bruce's lifetime would England be able to muster an effective invasion army, and immediate peace would have spared northern England some devastating raids.

There were peace negotiations, a long series of them, but they all split on the same rock, the recognition of Scottish independence. Edward, or the barons behind him, agreed that Bruce might keep his throne, but only as Regent for England. Tranquilly, but with unshaken determination, Bruce rejected all such offers. Scotland would be free, or there would be no peace.

If there was not actual peace, there was very little fighting. Several truce periods were arranged, some of them holding for as much as eighteen months. Although the fourteen years from Bannockburn to 1328 must be counted as war years, they were sufficiently calm to enable Bruce to reorganize his disordered kingdom and get on with the business of government.

Bruce's messages to his Parliament have a strangely modern ring. His task was the familiar one of reconversion to a peacetime economy. Scotch sheep produced an excellent grade of wool, but there were few facilities for turning it into cloth on a commercial scale. Most of the raw wool was exported to Flanders, whose textiles were famous all over Europe. The new Parliament passed laws favoring the immigration of Flemish weavers and merchants, granting them tax exemptions and other privileges. In the same way, Dutch shipbuilders were encouraged to settle in Scotland. This was the beginning of the great industries that make Scotch woolens and Scotch ships famous today.

Bruce's national defense program was equally simple and effective. Every able-bodied man worth ten pounds, provided he were not a priest or a monk, must provide himself with a suit of armor and a sword. If he were poorer, and owned no more than the value of a cow, he must possess a spear, or a bow with twenty-four arrows. At Easter-time every year, these men must present themselves to what amounted to a local draft board and demonstrate that they owned the weapons and knew how to use them. These "wapinschaws" took on the characteristics of Olympic games, with crowns of laurel for the best spearman or archer.

An energetic organizer of the wapinschaws was Walter Stewart, Douglas's handsome cousin. This young man, poet and perfect knight, came to be a popular member of the Bruce household. Even Queen Elizabeth, who was seldom pleased about anything, approved when he asked for Princess Marjorie's hand.

The young couple were married in the summer of 1315, less than a year after their first meeting. The union between two great Scottish houses was a suitable one, but there is no question that it was a love-match on both sides. This was so rarely the case in noble marriages that chroniclers of the day take pains to mention it. Bruce, whose first wife had been chosen for him by his father, and second by England's King, had never been granted the privilege of marrying for love. He was all the happier, therefore, to give his cherished daughter her heart's desire.

At the simple court he kept near Stirling, Bruce lived the life of a Scottish gentleman, with little of the pomp usually associated with royalty. His queen fretted a good deal about this, constantly nagging at him to build her a fine new house where she could preside in proper state. He good-naturedly promised to do so as soon as he had men and money to spare.

Men and money, while the war still dragged on, were too precious to spend on peacetime building. But Elizabeth was not the only person to have plans for spending them on an ambitious personal project.

A month after Princess Marjorie's wedding, Edward Bruce asked his brother for a private audience. He came to dinner, and after the meal was over Robert took him into his bedchamber, where they could be alone.

🌱 🌱 XX 🌱 🌱

In spite of the captured English tapestries masking the dank stone walls, the room was a cheerless one. Bruce took his place behind the massive table that served as his desk and motioned his brother to a chair near by.

"Well, Edward? You have an important matter to take up with me, you said. Let's hear it."

Edward Bruce produced a roll of parchment and flattened it out on the desk. "This came today, from the O'Neill of Ulster. I thought you ought to see it."

The King skimmed through the letter. Then, slowly and thoughtfully, he read it again. He laid it down and looked at his brother with a silent question in his eyes.

Edward flushed but answered the unspoken query with more than a touch of defiance.

"Yes, it's me they want, Robert! Why not? I have the same royal blood as you. You're already King of Scotland. Why shouldn't I be King of Ireland, if the Irish people want me? Is there anything wrong in that?"

"Nothing, Edward. Except the fact that they have no throne to bestow. Edward of England rules Ireland now."

"And a year ago he ruled Scotland!" Edward said impatiently. "You know yourself, Robert, that the Irish have suffered under English oppression ever since the Norman Conquest. They haven't had a king of their own since then, and they're a proud people. Why should they put up with it? Why shouldn't they win their freedom by the sword, as we Scots have done? Haven't they a right to it?"

"They have every right," Bruce agreed. "Surely you know, Brother, that I have always sympathized with the downtrodden Irish people. Their wrongs have been greater than ours, and more prolonged. I'm not disputing the justice of this cause."

"Well, then!" Edward's heavy face lighted with eagerness. "You can see for yourself what the O'Neill says. The people are ready to rise. All they need is a leader. A leader like me, he writes, a man who has already proved himself a match for the accursed English. They're waiting for me, Robert. And there's a crown to gain!"

"Perhaps. But it will not be an easy crown to gain, Edward. Have you thought of that?"

"Of course I've thought of it! I know it will mean

fighting, long hard fighting. But we've fought long and hard here, Robert. Do you think the Irish won't do the same?"

Bruce sighed. "I don't question the courage of the Irish, nor their patriotism. But I do not think they have the strength to oppose the English alone—no, not even under your leadership. O'Neill speaks here of Scottish soldiers, of arms and food and money. It would be a difficult and expensive business to make you King of Ireland, Brother."

"I knew it!" Edward brought his fist down on the table in an angry gesture. "Oh, I can see how it is. A hundred times I've heard you talk of the Irish and their wrongs. Always your heart was with them. But now, when they're ready to act, you hang back, you speak of difficulties. Perhaps, *your Majesty*," his mouth twisted into a sneer, "you would see it differently if they had offered their throne to *you*!"

All the Bruces had hot tempers. For a minute a dangerous quarrel was in the making. Then with a mighty effort the King controlled himself.

"I won't answer that taunt, Edward. It sounds as if you were my enemy, and I know well that you are not. You've served me loyally and well all these years, never asking a thing for yourself. We Scots have not seen the last of the English yet, and we can ill afford to divert men and resources to aid the Irish. But if you think such an enterprise has a chance of success, I will consent to it for your sake. I can't say more."

"Well, that's saying enough," Edward answered gruffly. "I spoke in haste just now, Robert. I'm sorry. You *will* consent, then?"

"If you wish it. You may not believe this," a smile of singular sweetness lighted Robert's rugged face, "but I'd like nothing better than to see my younger brother a brother king. I could only wish his chances were better."

"The chances aren't too bad," Edward said eagerly. "The Irish are boiling with resentment. Once I raise my banner on their soil they'll flock to me. And it will be a fine thing for Scotland, Robert. An independent Irish kingdom to stand beside you against the English—have you thought of that? And perhaps if God gives us children we'll arrange a cousin-marriage to unite the two states into one. That won't come about until after we're dead, though," he added hastily.

In spite of his worries, Bruce chuckled. Edward wanted so badly to be a king! Not even to the son he did not have would he relinquish the crown he had not yet won. Robert's recently married Marjorie was his only child, and Edward had none, but the suggestion of an Irish alliance against England was a welcome one. If

Edward could achieve it, it would be well worth the effort and expenditure involved. And it would be foolish to discount the brother's undoubted capacities, for he had proved them on many a battlefield.

Robert's heart was never in the Irish war. But, having consented to it, he gave Edward all the support he could possibly spare. An expedition was fitted out, and in May, 1316, Edward Bruce landed at Carricksfergus in Ulster. He was accompanied by Thomas Randolph and a small army, which was quickly swelled as the Irish chieftains joined him. His most powerful opponent was the Earl of Ulster, who was Queen Elizabeth's brother. Edward defeated the young Earl early in October and gained a strong foothold in northern Ireland.

In the first months all went well. One year after his landing, Edward imitated his brother Robert and held a coronation ceremony with a homemade crown. He had the support of the Irish nobles who had joined him, and of the Church dignitaries in that section. The affair was taken seriously enough for his name to appear in the history books as Edward I of Ireland. But he never ruled more than a small fraction of the country, and his hazardous reign did not long endure.

Immediately after his coronation, Edward sent Randolph home with an urgent message. Things were going splendidly in Ireland, but heavy reinforcements were

needed for the march on Dublin that would bring final
triumph. Edward implored his brother to send every
available man, and if possible to come himself. It would
be a fine spectacle for the people of Dublin, he wrote,
to see two kings enter their city in state.

Robert may have suspected that Edward's invitation
originated in a childish eagerness to show his brother
that he also was a king now. But from Randolph, who
had earned his own share of glory in the Irish war, he
learned that it was by no means certain that Dublin
would fall. The Irish nobles south of Ulster were bitterly
resisting his advance, preferring as they said to keep
their English slavery rather than exchange it for a Scottish one. It was less as a spectator than as a rescuer that
Robert was needed in Ireland.

Randolph came home to find his King so deeply distressed that he could scarcely bring his mind to political
matters. Only a month before, Princess Marjorie had
died in childbirth.

The baby who cost her her life, puny little Robert
Stewart, was one day to reign, the first of the long line
of Stewarts whose sorrows have been the tragedy of
Scotland. Unhappy Mary of Scots was descended from
Marjorie's child, and Bonnie Prince Charlie. From
Robert II also descended James VI of Scotland and I of
England, who three hundred bloody years later was to

heal the long breach and rule the United Kingdom of
Great Britain.

All the love of Bruce's lonely heart had gone out to
his daughter, so pitifully separated from him for most
of her life-span. Her death, a sudden lightning blow that
came without warning, left him inconsolable. Perhaps he
welcomed the opportunity to throw himself into the
Irish fighting and find forgetfulness. Leaving Douglas
and Walter Stewart as Guardians of the Realm, he sailed
for Ireland.

There he quickly found, as Randolph had warned
him, that his brother's optimism was wholly unjustified.
With the troops Robert had brought the two Kings moved
on Dublin but never came within sight of its steeples.
The resistance of the Irish earls was strengthened by a
newly arrived English army. The Bruces avoided open
defeat only by keeping out of contact with the enemy,
spending several wretched months in futile marches
across a famine-stricken, hostile land.

In March, 1317, Robert Bruce gave it up and went
home, taking his starving army with him. There are re-
ports of a furious quarrel between the brothers, but these
are not substantiated. Edward fought hopelessly on for
a few months more and met his death in a battle at Dun-
dalk. Enemy soldiers found his useless Irish crown when
they looted the baggage left in his stricken camp.

So ended the Irish adventure, a forlorn hope at best, and one destined by its very nature to fail. Robert Bruce had backed it reluctantly, and only because his brother urged it. Scottish blood and Irish blood flowed to no purpose, and only English interests profited by it. The cruel clutch of England tightened upon the hapless island, and Irishmen who loved freedom saw the last vestiges of it crushed in bloody reprisals.

Whether or not they parted in anger, Bruce mourned his brother's death deeply. Edward had stood at his side all through the early days, when his fortunes were at their lowest ebb. Very few of those early comrades remained to share the comparative tranquillity that wrapped the sore-tried land. Many had died in battle; more had known the shameful death that the English meted out to captive rebels. Bishop Lamberton remained, a fount of wise counsel, but he was growing very feeble. The older Bishop, Wishart, had lived to feel Scottish earth under his feet and then had thankfully closed his blind eyes in death. Stewart and Randolph, although dearly loved, were younger men who had not known the first bitter struggle. Of them all, only Douglas could look back to the beginning and share with his King the memories of the long road he had traveled.

The road was smoother now. Border fighting continued, but more and more Bruce left the active campaigning to Douglas and Randolph, while he devoted himself to the tedious tasks of peace. For the first time in his hard life, he had a semblance of domestic bliss. There was the little grandson to take Marjorie's place in his affections, and early in 1320 Elizabeth presented him with a daughter, christened Maude.

With two babies in the family, it was easy enough for the Queen to persuade her husband that the time had come to abandon antiquated Clackmannan Castle, with its arrow-slits for windows and its damp crumbling walls. He yielded to her coaxing and built her a handsome manor house on the bank of the River Clyde. The spot chosen was in easy reach of Perth, where Parliament met, but it was a country place, set in its own orchards and farmlands.

Cardross Manor, although stoutly built, lacked the fortifications that would have made it a castle. It was not a stronghold to defend but a house to live in. French and Dutch workmen came to line the airy chambers with fine wood paneling, to paint and gild and decorate at the Queen's direction. The windows were filled in with colored glass brought over from Venice, a luxury unheard of for a building that was not a church.

Elizabeth was delighted with her new home. The poor lady had never enjoyed many of the luxuries of royalty, although she had been a queen for so many years. She

built up a little court at Cardross and required her
ladies to curtsy after the English manner. She seldom
went to Perth but seemed content to stay in her new
house with its beautiful gardens. Her son, Prince David,
was born there. A year or two later she gave him a little
sister, Margaret.

❦ ❦ XXI ❦ ❦

EDWARD II OF ENGLAND was fast approaching his unhappy end. His new favorite, Hugh le Despenser, was a young man cut from the Piers Gaveston pattern, reckless and pleasure-loving, with no head for politics. But he had a father, Despenser the Elder, who was a capable statesman and who used his son's influence to take a hand in government. He might have proved a useful counselor, but the barons bitterly resented his interference. The lords and the Queen liked the Despensers even less than they had liked Gaveston, and all the old enmities flared again.

The situation was complicated by the introduction of a new personality. Queen Isabelle had acquired a favorite of her own, the husband of one of her ladies-in-waiting.

Roger Mortimer was twenty years older than Isabelle, a hard-bitten brutal, gangster type who is said to have won the Queen's affections by slapping her face. Whatever her reasons, she became madly infatuated with him and eagerly drew him into her plots against Edward.

227

All the plots and counterplots are hard to follow. Some of the nobles welcomed Mortimer as an ally, and others distrusted him. The Despensers, who had the King's ear, urged him to take strong measures against his enemies. He responded by arresting and executing the Earl of Lancaster, ringleader of the hostile Parliament.

This drastic action inflamed rather than quieted the growing turmoil. Mortimer's retainers, the private armed guard that every noble maintained, were a crew of ruffians who thought nothing of murder. Some of the lords' followers were no better. There were brawls in the streets, in the course of which innocent citizens were killed. Houses and shops were broken into, there were holdups in dark alleys, and law-abiding Londoners went in terror of their lives.

This breakdown of law and order alarmed the people, who did not know where to fix the blame. The sinister Mortimer so manipulated events that in the end they blamed their hapless King. He was insulted in Parliament and hooted in the streets. By the close of September, 1326, he had what amounted to a revolution on his hands. From all sides, pressure was being put upon him to abdicate and turn the throne over to his son. His very life was not safe, for he narrowly escaped poisoning at his own table.

The unhappy King turned for advice to the Despensers, as the only friends he could trust. At their suggestion he fled from London, taking Hugh le Despenser with him. He went to Wales, where he had been born, and where it was believed that the people still had some affection for him as their Prince.

The elder Despenser, left as governor of Bristol, was betrayed by his own garrison a week later. They handed him over to the barons, who promptly beheaded him.

Edward found his Welsh subjects unable or unwilling to defend him. He tried to go to Ireland, but stormy weather drove him back to Wales. The new Earl of Lancaster led an expedition across the Welsh border, and the King took to the hills. They found him cowering in a wayside chapel and took him back to England a prisoner. Hugh le Despenser, captured with him, was hanged, and his broken body fed to the London dogs.

The prisoner King was locked up in Kenilworth Castle, and Mortimer visited him there. What passed at the interview is not known, is best not guessed at. Roger Mortimer returned to London with a signed letter of abdication in which Edward yielded the throne to his fifteen-year-old son.

The abdication was greeted with heartfelt relief by practically everybody. Young Edward III was an intelligent, frank-hearted boy, very popular with the populace.

Since he was so young, a regency would be necessary, and both the barons and Mortimer expected that rich plum to fall into their hands. Everyone was happy except Queen Isabelle, who wanted to be a widow. Her friend Mortimer kindly obliged her.

Edward's murder was accomplished in a manner so fiendishly ingenious, so hideously revolting, that the details are omitted from most histories. It occurred at Berkeley Castle, but the aged and ailing Lord Berkeley had no hand in it. It was planned by Mortimer and carried out by two thugs whom he had foisted on Berkeley as jailers. Poor Edward's life held little to admire, and England was better off without him. But whatever his sins, he must have made full payment for them in the manner of his death.

The new regime did not work out exactly as planned. Edward III had inherited his mother's strength of will without her more despicable qualities. He managed to hold a nice balance between the barons and Mortimer, and as he grew older to assert his own wishes. None of the would-be advisers influenced him for long, and it is pleasant to report that the worst of them finally came to bad ends. Edward hanged Mortimer in 1330, and the wicked Queen lived out her wicked life a prisoner.

The most fortunate consequence of Edward III's accession was the ending of the Scottish war. The young

King made a couple of expeditions into Scotland, once narrowly escaping capture at Douglas's hands. He was soon convinced that there was no point in spending a lifetime, as his father had done, in the futile conflict. He consulted with the Pope, and new peace overtures were opened. There was a great deal of scurrying back and forth, and on May 4, 1328, the final peace treaty was signed.

The terms gave Scotland all that Bruce had fought for. He was recognized as King of an independent kingdom, owing no allegiance to England. The two countries bound themselves in a pact of everlasting friendship, to be symbolized by a union of the two reigning houses. Bruce's son, Prince David, was to take Edward's sister Joan as wife.

These dynastic marriages were a common feature of peace treaties and were based on sound reasoning. No human tie is stronger than the tie of blood. If anything could restrain a king from aggressive war against a neighbor, it should be the consideration that such a war was bound to injure his child, or his grandchildren. Of course it did not always work. Wars did break out, in spite of solemn promises cemented by family relationships. But if there is any infallible device for making peace treaties unbreakable, a war-weary world has not yet found it.

Little Joan Make-peace, as she was to be known in Scotland, was six years old. Prince David was four. It might seem that an engagement would be sufficient, and that the wedding could wait until the children were older. But an engagement can be broken, where a Catholic marriage cannot. For the sake of making the treaty most firmly binding, both sides felt it wise to hold the marriage ceremony without delay.

King Edward, among the rich gifts with which he dowered his little sister, generously offered one most acceptable to the groom's father. He used his good offices with the Pope to bring about a repeal of Bruce's excommunication, pronounced originally to please the first Edward. Although the decree had never been taken seriously in Scotland, it was a relief to everyone to have it lifted. Randolph went on a special mission to thank the Holy Father for his clemency, taking with him a handsome donation from Bruce to the papal Crusade fund.

In the autumn before the treaty was finally signed, Queen Elizabeth died at Cardross. Bruce mourned her with due decorum, giving her a costly funeral and founding a chaplainry at Cullen Abbey, that there might be perpetual prayers for the repose of her soul. She is buried at Dumfermline, where her husband lies beside her.

Since the motherless little Prince was soon to be a

bridegroom, his father revived the family title of Earl of Carrick for him and gave him Turnberry Castle.

A household was set up there, consisting of "a steward, a treasurer, nine ladies, five knights, three clerks, thirty-eight esquires and pages, nine chaplains, and appropriate servitors and garrison."

A little boy of four, even though he is a Prince-Earl and a husband, would need someone to teach him his ABC's and see that he washes behind the ears. Somewhere among that impressive retinue there must have been teachers and nurses, and perhaps a forthright Scotswoman empowered to spank when necessary. There is no record of any such arrangements. After all, royal dignity must be preserved.

The wedding was held at Berwick on July 19, 1328. Queen-Mother Isabelle, not yet fallen from favor, brought small Joan, with Mortimer heading the brilliant military escort. Douglas and Randolph, with the flower of the Highland regiments, accompanied David. The ceremony and the feast that followed it cost over a thousand pounds, a tremendous sum for those days. One hundred and seventy-one oxen were consumed at the feast, along with four hundred and thirteen sheep and fifty tuns of wine. English and Scottish knights who had striven grimly to kill each other in battle danced and sang and drank together in hilarious good fellowship.

Neither Edward of England nor Robert of Scotland was present to join in the festivities. The cause for Edward's absence is not known, but it was probably his growing dislike for Mortimer. It would hardly be possible to keep the bride's mother at home, and Isabelle went nowhere without her adored Roger. Perhaps Edward declared that if Mortimer went he would not go, and the Queen decided the issue.

Robert Bruce, absent also, was obliged to alter his plans at the last minute because of illness.

So far as we know, the Scottish King had been a well and hearty man ever since the "chill and fever" at Inverurie, twenty years before. Whatever malady afflicted him now came on suddenly, for he had fully intended to attend the wedding, even ordering himself a new gold chain to wear. This is one of the reasons why it is difficult to believe that the sickness which kept him from the wedding, and of which he died a year later, could be the dread thing the historians call it.

They say, all but one of them, that King Robert was a leper. He could have been. Leprosy is usually considered an Oriental disease, but the Crusades had spread it far and wide in the Europe of the Middle Ages. There were leper hospitals all over the continent, and in the British Isles. A special religious order, the Knights of Lazarus, had been formed to care for its victims. It was not impossible for Bruce to have contracted the disease. Only the circumstances of his latter days make it seem very improbable.

Leprosy as we know it does not strike one year and kill the next. Usually it is a long-drawn-out process of tissue breakdown, spread over some nine or ten years before it ends fatally. It is incredible that, if Robert had it, the fact was not known until the year before he died.

If he did have leprosy, and did know it, then it is equally incredible that he would have moved freely about the country or lived an ordinary family life. Medical men of his time believed not only that the disease was incurable but that it was so infectious that merely to stand in a leper's shadow was to incur his ailment. We know now that neither of these ideas is true, but Middle Age science held firmly to them.

Both church and civil law made strict provision for isolation. The sufferer confessed and received the last rites of the Church, as for a dying man. He was placed under a black canopy to simulate a coffin and led into the churchyard, where earth was cast over his feet. The priest blessed him for the last time, saying, "Be thou dead to man, but alive to God." His property passed to his heir, and he became a living dead man, barred from all human company but that of other lepers.

There is absolutely no suggestion that Robert Bruce passed through any such ordeal. He was the King, and he might have refused it. But the King's power ended at the church door. So afflicted, not a sovereign in Christendom would have dared to take his place in a congregation, nor would any priest have permitted it. We know that he did go to church, up to the last few weeks, when illness confined him to bed. Young David's wedding, which he had planned to attend, was solemnized in Berwick Cathedral.

To add to all this, there is the man's known character. He must have believed, like everyone else, that leprosy was virulently contagious. Yet he lived surrounded by his best friends, men like Douglas and Randolph, and his sisters and his young children. It is simply unthinkable that he would willfully have exposed those he loved best to such risk.

All these speculations are fruitless now. Like so many things about Robert Bruce, the nature of his illness will never be known. Whatever it was, it kept him from the wedding and made him an invalid for the few months that remained to him.

He was only fifty-four years old, but a French envoy who saw him for the first time took him for eighty. Nevertheless, he was up and about, sailing with Randolph on the Clyde, overseeing the re-roofing of his fal-

con-house, visiting the caged lion that an admirer had
sent him. In March, 1329, he set out with Douglas on a
sentimental pilgrimage to the old battlefields, but his
waning strength forced him to turn back. In May of that
year he took to his bed, never to rise again.

His closing days were tranquil ones. He knew quite
well that he was dying, and only one regret fretted him.

Long ago, before he took Scotland's woes upon his
shoulders, he had sworn a knightly vow to go to Palestine and wrest the Holy Sepulcher from the Moslems.
All young men who received their knighthood at Edward
I's hands took that vow, for Edward was an enthusiastic
Crusader. Bruce, with his hands full wresting Scotland
from England, had never had a chance to fulfill the vow
and probably had not thought of it for years. Now, as a
broken old man lay dying, the young knight's oath came
back to trouble him.

He eased his conscience by a device that does not
make sense to modern minds. We must remember that
the men of Bruce's day seriously considered the physical
heart to be the seat of all the higher emotions. We use
the word still in a figurative sense, but to them it was
real. Whatever a man felt of honor, of religion, of
patriotism and virtue, originated, they thought, in the
heart, the organ that we regard as simply a mass of
muscle located in the chest cavity. With this literal con-

ception in mind, Bruce's last wish seems reasonable and touching.

On June 7, 1329, he summoned his family and friends about his bedside. The little Earl of Carrick was lifted to a stool. Then, because he was so small in that crowd of burly Scotsmen, the King motioned feebly to Randolph.

"Raise him up, Tommie. Set the laddie high on your shoulder, that all may see their King."

In simple, broken words, then, he took his last farewell of those who had served him and their country. His worn face brightened into smiles as the chiefs knelt and swore fealty to little King David.

"And Thomas Randolph, too, if it is your will," Bruce went on. "He is my choice to rule for the little one until he comes to manhood. But I would not force you, my friends. You know I've never wanted to do that. Will you have Randolph for your regent?"

Without a dissenting murmur they knelt before Randolph and repeated the oath.

"And now—" Bruce's voice was failing. Where he waited in the shadows, a young priest started forward. Old Bishop Lamberton was lately dead, and Bruce's confessor now was the fighting chaplain of the Carrick clan. Bruce pressed his hand affectionately.

"Not yet, Father," he whispered. "Jamie, come closer."

Douglas, weeping noisily and not ashamed of it, stooped his great length over the bed. In painful gasps the King gave his last commands. His body was to lie in Dumfermline Abbey, ancient tomb of Scottish kings. But, "seeing that my body cannot go to achieve what my heart desires," the heart itself was to be taken to Jerusalem, there to rest in the Holy Sepulcher, "that it may lie where our Lord lay."

Douglas, choking with sobs, accepted the trust. Then, at the chaplain's imperative gesture, they all withdrew and left the dying man to make his peace with God.

He died, comforted and at ease, toward evening. The body was buried at Dumfermline. With the embalmed heart in a silver casket, James Douglas set out for the Holy Land. Several of Bruce's most devoted knights went with him.

Douglas, meaning to make his way to the East by way of Spain, never left Spanish soil. King Alfonso was embroiled in a war with the Moors of Granada, and Good Lord James could never resist a fight. With his knights he plunged into the battle, and fell pierced by Moorish steel. Sir William Keith, although wounded himself, managed to take the casket from Douglas's body. He carried the heart back to Scotland, where it rests in Melrose Abbey.

So ends the story of King Robert the Bruce. When all the bits of fact have been patiently disentangled from the mass of myth and legend, when due allowance is made for the venomous spite of enemies and the idolatrous exaggerations of friends, it is not so romantic a story as the poets would have it. Yet out of it all the man emerges, stark and strong, a man of whom Scotland does well to be proud.

Once, when the Pope threatened to excommunicate every man who followed him, the Scottish Parliament answered with a letter in which the chiefs gave their own estimate of Robert Bruce. It is a fitting description of the man, and of the spirit with which he inspired his countrymen.

"Our lord and Sovereign, Robert, . . . gladly endured toil, pain, the extremity of want and every danger to save his people and kingdom from their enemies. By reason of his desert as of his rights, the Providence of God, the lawful succession which we will maintain with our lives, and our common and just consent, have made him our King, because through him our salvation has been wrought. . . . We fight not for glory nor for wealth nor honor, but for that freedom which no good man surrenders but with his life."

❦ ❦ Bibliography ❦ ❦

Adams, Frank. *The Clans, Septs and Regiments of the Scottish Highlands.* Edinburgh: W. & A. K. Johnston, Ltd., 1925.

Anonymous. *Scottish Clans and their Tartans.* Edinburgh: W. & A. K. Johnston, Ltd., 1906.

Brown, P. Hume. *History of Scotland.* Cambridge, England: University Press, 1899.

Calthrop, Dion Clayton. *English Costume.* London: Adam and Charles Black, 1906.

Clay, Rotha Mary. *The Medieval Hospitals of England.* London: Methuen & Co., 1909.

Cornish, F. Warre. *Chivalry.* London: Swan Sonnenschein & Co., Lim., 1908.

Hume, David. *History of England.* New York: The Publishers' Plate Renting Co., (no date).

Ker, J. Inglis. *Scotland for the Motorist.* New York: Charles Scribners' Sons, 1928.

Kerr, Robert. *History of Scotland during the Reign of Robert I, surnamed The Bruce.* Edinburgh: Brown & Crombie, 1811.

Linklater, Eric. *Robert the Bruce.* New York: D. Appleton-Century Company, 1934.

Mackay, J. G. *The Romantic Story of the Highland Garb and the Tartan.* Stirling, Scotland: Eneas Mackay, 1924.

Mackenzie, Agnes Mure. *The Kingdom of Scotland.* London: W. & R. Chambers, Ltd., 1940.

————. *Robert Bruce, King of Scots.* London: Alexander Maclehose & Co., 1934.

Mackie, R. L. *Story of Robert the Bruce.* London: George G. Harrop & Company, 1913.

Maxwell, Sir Herbert. *Robert the Bruce.* New York: G. P. Putnam's Sons, 1897.

Maxwell, Sir John Stirling. *Shrines and Homes of Scotland.* London: Alexander Maclehose & Co., 1937.

Norris, Herbert. *Costumes and Fashion.* London: J. M. Dent & Sons, Ltd., 1927.

Patmore, K. A. *The Seven Edwards of England.* London: Methuen & Co., Ltd., 1911.

Porter, Jane. *The Scottish Chiefs* (Fiction). New York: Charles Scribners Sons, (no date).

Scott, Sir Walter. *Tales of a Grandfather.* New York: Frederick A. Stokes Company, (no date).

Scott-Moncrieff, George. *The Stones of Scotland.* London: B. T. Batsford, Ltd., 1938.

Catholic Encyclopedia.
Encyclopedia Britannica, 9th edition.
Encyclopedia Britannica, 14th edition.
New Standard Encyclopedia.

Index

243